T0360471

Bear Traps on Russia's Road to Modernization

Bear Traps on Russia's Road to Modernization examines Russia's longer term economic growth prospects. It argues that Russia's growth challenges are conventionally misdiagnosed and examines the reasons why: a spatial misallocation that imposes excess costs on production and investment; distortions to human capital; an excessively high relative price of investment that serves as a tax on physical capital accumulation; and an economic mechanism that inhibits adjustments that would correct the misallocation. *Bear Traps on Russia's Road to Modernization* explains why Soviet legacies still constrain economic growth and outlines a feasible policy path that could remove these obstacles.

The most popular proposals for Russian economic reform today—diversification, innovation, modernization—are misguided. They are based on a faulty diagnosis of the country's ills, because they ignore a simple reality: Russia's capital, both physical and human, is systematically overvalued, owing to a failure to account for the handicap imposed by geography and location. Part of the handicap is an unavoidable consequence of Russia's size and cold climate. But another part is self-inflicted. Soviet policies placed far too much economic activity in cold, remote locations. Specific institutions in today's Russia, notably its federalist structure, help preserve the Soviet spatial legacy. As a result, capital remains handicapped.

Investments made to compensate for the handicaps of cold and distance should properly be treated as costs. Instead, they are considered net additions to capital. When returns to what appear to be large quantities of physical and human capital fail to satisfy expectations, the blame naturally goes to poor institutions, corruption, backward technology, and so on. Policy proceeds along the wrong path, with costly programs that can end up doing more damage than good. The authors insist that the goal should be to seek to remove the handicaps rather than to spend to compensate for them. They discuss how Russia could develop a modernization program that would let the nation finally focus on its economic advantages, not its handicaps.

Clifford G. Gaddy is Senior Fellow at the Brookings Institution, USA, and Scientific Adviser, CRIFES.

Barry W. Ickes is Professor of Economics at The Pennsylvania State University, USA, and Director of CRIFES.

Bear Traps on Russia's Road to Modernization

Clifford G. Gaddy and
Barry W. Ickes

Routledge
Taylor & Francis Group

LONDON AND NEW YORK

First published 2013
by Routledge
2 Park Square, Milton Park, Abingdon, Oxon OX14 4RN

Simultaneously published in the USA and Canada
by Routledge
605 Third Avenue, New York, NY 10017

Routledge is an imprint of the Taylor & Francis Group, an informa business

British Library Cataloguing in Publication Data
A catalogue record for this book is available from the British Library

Library of Congress Cataloging in Publication Data
Gaddy, Clifford G.
Bear traps on Russia's road to modernization / Clifford G. Gaddy and
Barry W. Ickes.
  pages cm
  1. Russia (Federation)–Economic policy–1991- 2. Sustainable
  development–Russia (Federation) I. Ickes, Barry William. II. Title.
  HC340.12.G328 2013
  338.947'07–dc23

ISBN: 978-0-415-66275-8 (hbk)
ISBN: 978-0-415-66276-5 (pbk)

Typeset in Times New Roman
by Sunrise Setting Ltd, Paignton, UK

Contents

Figures

Tables

Preface

Russia is often treated as a mystery or puzzle. This applies not least to the realm of economic policy. When economic outcomes do not accord with expectations, and especially when those outcomes run counter to policy advice, observers often invoke a special "Russian way" or some other variety of irrationality as explanations. These convenient crutches, however, do not increase our understanding. An alternative approach to studying Russia is to begin by assuming that Russians are as rational as anyone else, and then to consider what the constraints are that would lead rational agents to make the choices they do. The research that forms the core of this book follows in the tradition of searching for such constraints, with emphasis on identifying the structural legacies from which the constraints are derived. Our goal has been to discern the extent to which Russia's seemingly puzzling outcomes can be explained by a deeper understanding of the legacies of the Soviet period.

This volume began to take shape when we received a grant from the Smith Richardson Foundation to produce a report on the medium-term growth prospects of Russia. That report formed the basis of the book. We are especially grateful to Nadia Schadlow for her guidance and support. Our research could not have been conducted without the generous financial support of the Human Capital Foundation to CRIFES at the Pennsylvania State University. We are also grateful to colleagues from the Institute of Financial Studies in Moscow for their support of this research.

We thank the editors at Routledge and three anonymous reviewers for their comments on early drafts of this manuscript. We are grateful to Konstantin Kucheravyy for research assistance.

Introduction

This is a book about the prospects for modernization of the Russian economy. Most such analyses focus on the will to reform: if only the country's leaders were sufficiently committed to reform, Russia could be modernized. Our approach, by contrast, assumes a Russia in which modernizers rule. They have the power to pursue reform and are fully committed to it. Our focus is on what happens next: specifically, on the difficulty that arises when these committed reformers improperly diagnose the problem. We argue that virtually all those who have presented plans for reforming Russia resemble the well-meaning physician who plans to cure the seriously ill patient by applying state of the art knowledge but with an improper diagnosis of the problem. We are not arguing that the well-meaning physician is using leeches because of a lack of medical knowledge. We are arguing that using the best frontier treatments and therapies will still have adverse consequences if they are treating the wrong disease. Hence, our emphasis in this book is on failure to diagnose properly.

Russia seems to be engaged in a perpetual search for the sources of sustainable economic growth. As so often in the past, discussions of "modernization," "innovation," and "diversification" are popular now in Russia. The chief sponsor of such ideas over the past few years has been former president, now prime minister, Dmitry Medvedev, who argues that Russia's resource-based economy is primitive and noncompetitive. Reactions to Medvedev's call for modernization have varied. Some thought earlier, and still do think, that it represents a great hope to resume serious reform of the Russian economy and politics. Others were cynical and see the return of Vladimir Putin to the presidency as confirmation that reform will never happen. But virtually all agree that Medvedev was correct in saying that if his modernization program were to be successful, it would be wonderful for Russia.

Our reaction is different. We think it most likely that under the specific Russian circumstances pertaining today, a modernization program would lead to negative results. This is because none of the modernization programs currently being discussed take into account the real reasons for Russia's backwardness. We argue that there are two main causes. The first is the inherited production structure – both the particular kinds of physical and human capital that were accumulated in the Soviet era and the manner in which they were allocated, including their spatial allocation. The second is the condition we call rent addiction, which means that there is an imperative to distribute a large share of Russia's oil and gas rents to the production enterprises that employ this inherited physical and human capital. Any "modernization" policy that fails to address the problem of addiction will simply distribute more rents to the addicts. Far from truly modernizing Russia, it will only reinforce the backwardness and inefficiency.

Herein lies the tragedy. Russia does need to move on a path towards sustainable growth, but unless the policies to achieve that goal are chosen with full recognition of the real causes of stagnation and backwardness – rent addiction and the structural legacy it helps perpetuate – the policies will likely lead to even worse problems in the future. They appear to lead to the goal but in fact lead into traps. Our purpose in this work is to warn against such mistaken and misinformed policies by identifying and analyzing the specific conditions for Russia's backwardness. Because they are specifically Russian – rooted in Russia's geography, notably its vast size and resource abundance, and its history – we call them "bear traps."

Russia is a resource-dependent economy, and its addiction to resource rents is the most important feature of its political economy. We have dealt at length with this issue in our book (Gaddy and Ickes forthcoming) and in a series of articles (see, for example, Gaddy and Ickes 2013). Hence, for the purposes of this study we will take the problem of resource dependence and addiction as a given feature of the environment as we examine the bear traps that Russia faces. As we examine the consequences of Russia's inherited structure for its economic future we must not forget that it is the abundance of resource rents that makes it possible to preserve the inherited production structure and its distortions and that it is the addictive nature of Russia's relationship with these rents that provides the mechanism for its preservation.

Typically the problems of the Russian economy manifest themselves in a distorted way. In Soviet times outside analysts examined data on the economy with great caution, owing to the hurdles presented by central planning. Although central planning is dead and Russia has a market economy now, the need for caution remains. There are three primary reasons for this. First are Russia's specific geographical peculiarities: space and cold. Russia is by territory the largest country in the world, by far, and it is also by far the coldest country in the world. In no other country do these factors present such actual and potential obstacles to economic activity as in Russia. Capital and labor are handicapped in ways that make their productivity and hence their value often quite different than they appear.

Second, there are legacies from the Soviet period that continue to distort our picture. In the Soviet period the price system that acted as a prism producing a "circus mirror effect," where relative prices made loss-making manufacturing enterprises seem productive and made the resource sectors seem to be only modest contributors to prosperity. The Soviet price system is history, but the legacy of decisions made in the Soviet period continues to have effects. In particular, many of these legacies lead to an overvaluation of assets and consequently to an underestimation of the rate of return on those assets. This is not, primarily, a statistical issue; rather, it is a failure to take into account the legacy of misallocation and inherited structure. This leads both to overestimation of assets and failure to recognize that legacies are the real problem. This is the ultimate bear trap.

Third, resource abundance exacerbates the legacies from central planning. It has led to addiction through production, creating an economic structure that is dependent on infusions of value from the resource sector. It also allows the pursuit of misguided policies for longer periods of time than would otherwise be the case. In addition, the under-appreciation of the role of resources leads to a fundamental misdiagnosis of Russia's economic health. This arises from the way that real output is measured, in particular real gross domestic product (GDP), which, in turn, is often used in analyzing movements in the economy. Growth in real GDP is measured as the change in output at unchanged prices.[1] The impact of prices is intentionally filtered out. This sensible procedure becomes problematic when a resource-abundant economy experiences a shock to the price of its resources.

Consider, for example, what would happen if oil prices boomed and oil output remained constant (say, to maintain export quotas and market share). Real output of the oil sector would thus be unchanged, providing no contribution to aggregate GDP growth. National income would rise, of course, owing to the increased prices of exports. And since this income is utilized in the economy, we would expect output to rise in the non-oil sector. Hence, we would measure a rise in real GDP – but none of this would occur in the oil sector. Now suppose that we have performed a growth accounting exercise to explain the sources of growth in this period. With real GDP growing but the impact of oil excluded, the only feasible explanations are growth in primary input use (capital and/or labor) or growth in total factor productivity (TFP).[2] To the extent that we observe growth in TFP (the more likely outcome), we are likely to conclude that:

- The economy became more efficient, causing the Solow residual to increase, or;
- Innovation and technology modernization have become a key source of growth.

Clearly, however, neither of these conclusions is warranted, and they are counterproductive as inputs to policy analysis. Both conclusions suggest that less emphasis on the resource sector could be valuable for long-term growth. But the true source of growth in this example, by construction, was precisely the resource boom. Hence, the accounting exercise has pushed our focus in the wrong direction.

The key problem in Russia is the systematic misuse of assets. For all the reasons we have just discussed, effective input levels of capital and labor services are mismeasured. The actual levels are below the measured levels. This leads to a misdiagnosis of Russia's maladies. Because the input levels are systematically overstated, the returns on investments in physical and human capital appear to be systematically below what they should be. The conclusion is that the key Russian problems relate to efficiency, primarily organizational, and perhaps also corruption.

We argue, on the contrary, that diagnosis must begin with a correct measurement of the input levels. If we could account for the overstatement of inputs, the picture would be different. We refer to the degree of mismeasurement as the τ-factor.[3] The idea is that if measured capital and labor services are L and K, respectively, the actual effective values are $\tau_L L$ and $\tau_K K$, where $\tau_L, \tau_K < 1$. These are discount factors that ought to be applied to measure the actual factor services used in Russia. Our goal in this book is to explain the causes and magnitudes of these discount factors and the implications for economic policy and performance when they are ignored. As we will show, the fundamental obstacle to correct policy is failure to write down the value of assets to eliminate the distortion caused by the τ-factor.

A useful allegory to elucidate our thesis is that of the *scrapping problem*. Consider the investment dilemma of a business faced with a fundamental technological revolution in its industry. The business has invested heavily in the old technology over the years. Its activity is thoroughly dependent on that old technology. The company must choose between upgrading the old technology or scrapping it entirely and fully re-equipping with the new technology. The two technologies are incompatible. It is an "all-or-nothing" choice. Nothing of the existing capital stock can be re-employed.

It also cannot be sold to help finance the new acquisition. The first path – upgrading – is cheaper and produces results immediately, but it locks the company into a second-rate path. No matter how much the old technology is upgraded, continuing to depend on it will ultimately doom the company to noncompetitiveness. The second approach is very costly up-front. It requires shutting down operations for a period. New staffing will be required. A few employees can retrain, but most cannot.

Structurally, Russia (in types of industry and in location) is like this company that made the "wrong" technology choice long ago. Because of the poor governance of that company in the past, it ignored all the signals indicating that the choice was wrong. Rather, over time it concentrated even more on the wrong path.[4] In the market economy, when market value falls too far below the historical value you recognize the mistake, and disinvest – write down the investment – because you have no choice. But in the Soviet system this feedback was not there. There was no force correcting the mistakes.

This company ended up on the verge of collapse, so new management took over. The new managers correctly recognized that the current disastrous state of the corporation was fundamentally due to the management practices of the past, so they changed the governance procedures in order to ensure that future business decisions will be rational and efficiency-enhancing. The problem is that as they focus on a real problem – the old system of management and decision-making in the company – the new managers ignore the problem of the inherited antiquated technology. They fail to see that they will never be able to rehabilitate the company unless they can successfully rid the company of the single biggest mistake caused by the old management system: the commitment to the wrong technology. And so, working hard to introduce correct new management practices, they work to "improve" the company's inherited capital stock – the capital that is all based on the wrong technology. They do the "right" things in the "right" way … with the wrong capital. They are doomed to fail.

The question is why would new owners be unwilling to write down the value of the assets and restructure? Why do they maintain the old technology? The key point is that transparently recognizing that the market value of the enterprise is much lower than that which it is believed to be can be disadvantageous to critical stakeholders. We develop this point in more detail in Chapter 4, on the political economy of federalism.

The first direction of our investigation will thus focus on physical assets, capital. In Chapter 2 we investigate how capital is systematically over-valued in Russia. Investment represents the sacrifice of current consumption for future benefits, but, as we will demonstrate, Russia receives far less future benefit than its sacrifice implies. The primary reason for this is that conventional ways to account for capital accumulation do not take into account features of space and cold. In Chapter 3 we examine how the legacy of the location policies pursued in Soviet times produced this handicap. The analysis of Chapters 2 and 3 presents a dilemma, however. If cold and space are such handicaps to growth, why are they not removed by investment policies? That is, why doesn't a market economy undo the location decisions of the Soviet period and cause the distribution of population to move towards the warmer parts of Russia? We try to answer this question in Chapter 4, where we focus on the implications of federalism in Russia. Our analysis shows that federalism "Russia style" leads to an immobilization of factors. There is, in fact, a political imperative to "keep the lights on" – that is, to keep factories running and people in place to man them – in what ought to become the ghost regions of Russia. We then turn to an analysis of the other important factor for growth, human capital, in Chapter 5. The problems of Russia's demography and its health crisis are well known. The important question, however, is how important these issues are to Russia's economic future: we argue in Chapter 5 that the emphasis on these problems misses the key point. As with physical capital, human capital is mismeasured in Russia. There is a τ-factor regarding labor as well, and a failure to recognize this can lead to another bear trap, another barrier to long-term Russian growth.

Bear traps thus arise because of the failure to recognize the implications of the τ-factor. The real goal of Russian policy should be to eliminate the impact of the τ-factor. It is important to emphasize that τ is not a measure of ignorance. It is the result of a systematic overvaluation of assets. The τ-factor is not unique to Russia. But, owing to the peculiarities of Russia's climate, location, and history, its impact is greater there than in other countries, and the risk of misdiagnosis of Russia's maladies is correspondingly greater. The misdiagnosis leads to faulty policies which invariably waste resources and, in the worst case, may even make the real problems worse. A prime example is the attention given to corruption as a main cause of Russia's inefficiency. Overvaluation of assets makes TFP in Russia appear very low. This is just a feature of arithmetic. But the interpretation of low TFP is that corruption and general inefficiency are the prime culprits. This is not to argue that corruption is not an important problem in Russia, but while the emphasis stays on corruption and general inefficiency, the impact of the legacies is ignored. And this leads to bear traps.

Not all of the special factors associated with Russia's legacy are immutable. Much is self-induced. Physical geography cannot be changed, but economic geography can be. Where you choose to locate economic activity is endogenous. Calls for modernization and diversification ignore the benefits of Russia's geography and fail to recognize how the τ-factor is going to make diversification truly difficult. In our concluding chapter, we examine potential economic futures for Russia, but in the context of what is actually feasible, based on our previous analysis. We argue that Russia should take advantage of its resources (whose location is part of its physical geography) but minimize the negative effects of geography by moving non-resource industries into regions that are warmer and closer to markets.[5]

1   Historical prelude

We stressed in the previous chapter that bear traps arise when policymakers misdiagnose the problems they are trying to solve. To set the stage for the analysis that follows, it is useful to consider the single most serious error in diagnosis, the one that led to the preservation of the Soviet legacy and thus to all the bear traps that we study. This is the error in diagnosing the fundamental reasons for the collapse of the Soviet economy. This misdiagnosis led to the implementation of an inappropriate therapeutic regime and thereby created the environment for the political–economic system that followed.

The Soviet economy was driven by resource rents. The value created from resources allowed an inherently inefficient industrial structure to be built that could be sustained only through continued infusion of value. The economy was like an inverted funnel: the resource sectors were the narrow neck of the funnel, and from them rent was distributed to a broad base. When resource rents collapsed in the second half of the 1980s, the Soviet economy collapsed with it.[1] The common diagnosis, however, was that the centrally planned economy's demise was not about the inherent inefficiency of the production structure; rather, it was due to inefficient organization and perverse incentives. If those could be improved, the economy would eventually prosper. In other words, the diagnosis was that the capital in the inherited structure was fine; the problem was the organization of production. As a result, at the critical moment of collapse there was no write-down of the assets of the Soviet legacy. The industrial structure that had been built and supported by resource rents was not shrunk to size.

The therapy prescribed on the basis of the misdiagnosis of the problem was privatization of the formerly state-owned production apparatus. Politically, the best way to achieve this was mass privatization: each citizen would be given a share of the existing assets. The basic principle would be to let each worker have a share of the enterprise in which he or she worked. People thought this made sense; they presumed that the places where they worked were legitimate value-producing enterprises. Granted, there was great concern that these assets would not be shared fairly – that the bosses would be able to manipulate the process and get too much at the expense of ordinary workers – but few doubted that the assets to be privatized were valuable.

Privatization was thus viewed as a redistribution of assets whose value was evident to all involved. We suggest, however, that what actually went on in Russia's privatization process was not a sharing of the nation's property, but a lottery in which all participants were given tickets whose value was known to only a few. There were a very small number of winning tickets, worth billions of dollars, and a huge number of losing tickets, worth nothing at all.[2] The winning tickets were shares in the resource-producing firms and the losing tickets were those in most manufacturing enterprises, among others. Describing Russian privatization as a lottery is consistent with the true diagnosis of the Russian economy, one that recognizes that legacies of cold and distance to market had made too many enterprises into dinosaurs incapable of surviving in a new environment.

The winners of the lottery could not allow the privatization process to be exposed as a lottery, nor could they afford to enforce the strict outcome of the lottery. A Russia in which a handful of people obtained all the wealth in the country would be politically unacceptable and would create a backlash that would lead to re-nationalization of all assets. The winners therefore needed to create the illusion that the losing tickets had some value. They did this by transferring some of their rents to the manufacturing sectors via the transfer mechanisms we referred to as "Russia's Virtual Economy." This had the benefit of concealing the true outcome, allowing many Russians to continue to believe that the manufacturing plants produced value. And, because people were suffering so much, it did not require a large quantity of resources to keep the plants running.

The Virtual Economy preserved the illusion that the economy was not the inverted funnel that a proper diagnosis would have revealed. But it did not prevent the lottery winners – the so-called oligarchs – from engaging in fighting amongst themselves. Their internecine battle for wealth was wasteful and potentially self-destructive. Vladimir Putin posed a way out for the oligarchs, through an arrangement we have referred to as Putin's Protection Racket (Gaddy and Ickes 2010). This arrangement accomplishes two key tasks:

- It protects the oligarchs from each other.
- It protects the oligarchs from the holders of losing tickets.

In exchange for this dual protection the oligarchs are obliged to share the resource rents with the dinosaur manufacturing sectors and, by so doing, they maintain the myth that the assets in those sectors produce value and do not need to be written off. Putin, the oligarchs, the governors of the regions, and the workers all share an interest in preserving the myth of the productivity of this fictitious capital. The current political economy of Russia – its rent management system – was thus born out of the original misdiagnosis. If it had been recognized at the start of transition that the nonproductive assets had no value and if there had been a write-down of those assets, the legacies would have been minimized and bear traps avoided. As it happened, the bear traps were set.

2 Investment and physical capital

Introduction

Properly conceived, investment is the essence of the process of creating a market economy. This point needs to be stressed, because transitions from Soviet-style planned economies to market economies have typically been thought of as a matter of "re-writing the rules" – that is, adopting new legal codes and establishing the institutions to enforce them. By that understanding, progress in transition is measured by what is still missing among the rules and the institutions. But the big problem for Russia is not what is missing, but rather what has been left behind by the old economy as a result of 70 years of misallocation under the old rules. The real task of transition is to unmake and rebuild that old economy: in other words, investment. All else is prelude.

Investment decisions can be analyzed as a sequence of two steps: the first step is to determine the gap between the desired and actual capital stock; the second is to choose the optimal path to close this gap. Much of the analysis of investment in Russia downplays the first step and implicitly focuses on the second, emphasizing such determinants as corporate governance and corruption. In the case of Russia, however, the first step is particularly critical. There are important misperceptions with regard to both the actual and desired capital stocks. On the one hand, the actual capital stock in Russia is overstated, owing to a failure to write down to market. On the other hand, the desired capital stock is underestimated because of an unwillingness to recognize the distance to market (that is, the competitiveness of Russian capital).[1] In this chapter we examine the forces that lie behind these two tendencies to misestimate the preconditions for the investment problem.

The ironic situation of the Russian economy is that while changing the rules, and even the institutions, of the economy will not make many of its assets profitable to use in a market economy, agents still prefer to keep them in operation. This represents an important puzzle about the Russian economy.[2] Moreover, it is the continued operation of many of the enterprises that control these assets that makes the price of investment goods in Russia extraordinarily high when measured at international prices.[3] This means that the increment to productive capacity that Russia gets for its investment effort is low compared with other countries, including transition economies. In general, a high relative price of investment can be due to distortions that raise the prices of investment goods or it may be the result of the relative efficiency of the production of consumption goods, as is the case in poorer countries. We argue below that in the case of Russia it is primarily problems on the investment side that dominate.

Why is Russia's investment problem underestimated? One reason is that the inherited capital stock from Soviet times was so large. Since the Soviets overinvested for 70 years, one might logically ask, how could underinvestment be the problem now? Underinvestment now could, in fact, be a healthy phenomenon, since it might reflect decisions not to continue wasteful investment patterns of the past. But this misses a fundamental point. The Soviet Union did not just overinvest in a general sense; it misinvested. That is, it built and installed the wrong kinds of capital, and it located this capital in the wrong places. As a result, the actual and market value of the inherited capital stock is low. The depreciation of the capital stock caused by liberalization and the transition to the market economy is, in fact, disinvestment. Hence, the market value of the capital stock at the start of transition was far below its notional value.[4]

Yet, when people speak of investment needs, they most often refer to what it would take to make existing physical configurations viable. These analysts assume that the capital stock itself is fine, but the problem is with the institutional and organizational context within which this capital is employed. This is not the correct way to view the issue, because it takes Soviet investment decisions as the correct base to build on. Nonetheless, it is a characteristic way of viewing the problem, and we will focus on this.

The preceding discussion suggests that we can distinguish two views about investment in Russia. The conventional view is that the main barriers to investment are currently institutional – an inadequate financial system, poor corporate governance, an excessive tax burden, and the like. All this makes the risk premium too high right now to invest in non-energy sectors. However, once the institutional reforms are implemented, investment will flow to non-energy sectors of the economy.[5] The alternative view is that investment in non-energy sectors is constrained by low potential: the capital–labor bundles are too inefficient.[6] By this line of reasoning, even if investment in energy were to be satiated investment would not flow to the non-energy sectors. In this second view it is the internal aspects that are critical, not the external, institutional, aspects.

Not surprisingly, the policy implications of these two views of investment differ. The main implications of the conventional view are obvious: continue with institutional reforms. For the alternative view, the policy implications are more complex. On the surface it might seem that, at a minimum, it is at least fine to continue with the same kind of institutional reforms as dictated by the conventional view. True, those institutional reforms might not solve the problem. But they cannot hurt. But, in fact, it is never enough to say that an action is worth taking simply because it has benefits. Policy-making is a costly endeavor, and one must therefore always consider the alternatives. Prioritizing institutional reforms might divert scarce political as well as monetary resources away from more important and urgent tasks. In Russia, bureaucratic competence is a scarce resource.[7]

The real policy problem of the alternative view is what, if anything, can be done to change the true investment attractiveness of the non-energy sectors? Herein lie some dangers. The critical issue is to distinguish between investments to improve technical efficiency and those to improve allocative efficiency. Technical efficiency refers to obtaining more output from given inputs. Allocative efficiency is achieving optimal outcomes given available resources; it compares how resources are allocated across activities.[8] Even miraculous improvements in technical efficiency (which will almost certainly be quite costly) may not be enough to compensate for the fundamental mistakes in allocative efficiency that today's Russia inherited from the Soviet Union. The practical problem for policymakers can be put simply: Do you encourage investment to make economic activity in Novosibirsk (or Chelyabinsk, or Perm) more productive, or do you channel that investment into a Western oblast that may have better economic fundamentals?[9]

Is investment a problem in Russia?

The Soviet period demonstrated that very high investment rates were no guarantee against stagnant and even decreasing growth rates. As we have suggested, this led many observers to de-emphasize the role of investment rates[10] and to focus instead on organizational improvements and other elements of economic reform as the crucial factors for growth. The implicit assumption is that inherited inefficiency takes the form of production well within efficiency frontiers, and that privatization and other institutional reforms can lead to rapid improvements in productivity growth. A clear example of this view was offered by Palmeda and Lewis:[11]

> There are no natural or economic obstacles to high economic growth in Russia, and the current situation need not be tolerated. Russia can rely on a skilled and inexpensive labor force, large and economically

attractive energy reserves, and surprisingly, much spare capacity in potentially productive industrial assets. Explicit and targeted social policies combined with balanced and enforceable regulations (mostly at the sector level, involving taxes, energy, land and red tape) would remove the most important market distortions. The payoff would be strong economic growth in Russia. (Palmeda and Lewis 2001: 49)

While organizational improvements are important, this view ignores the fact that the capital stock Russia inherited from the Soviet period is highly inefficient and may not be competitive even with frontier management. This is partly the result of investment decisions which were based on artificially low prices for energy and other inputs and which largely ignored the costs of the cold and location. Moreover, the enterprises that manufacture inefficient producer goods present a continued handicap to the growth process, as outlined below.[12]

New versus installed capital

Especially in transition, it is crucial to distinguish the returns from installed and new capital. Installed capital – the inherited capital stock from the Soviet period – is highly inefficient. New capital, by contrast, can offer high returns, precisely because it can be made appropriate to new economic circumstances. The problem is how to guarantee that new investment is appropriate in that sense and that it does not merely replenish depreciated capital stuck in the wrong places. "New" capital that simply replaces the obsolete or worn-out capital inherited from the Soviet economy is not new at all. Assuming that incentives can be structured so that investment is appropriate, the question then becomes: How much investment does Russia require? Is Russia investing enough? To answer this question, we first turn to the lessons from empirical growth analysis.

Growth models and Russian growth

Recent literature on the sources of economic growth underscores the importance of investment. In their benchmark study Ross Levine and David Renelt (1992) concluded that, despite the dozens of policy or institutional variables that have been hypothesized to account for growth, the only truly robust correlation was that between growth and the share of a nation's output that was devoted to investment, the so-called investment share of GDP. Their work spurred a number of subsequent efforts to analyze the prospects for long-term growth, including in countries making a transition from a central planning system to a market economy. All of these studies confirm the same basic lesson: the key robust correlate of growth is investment. Such analyses typically proceed from some form of the original Levine–Renelt growth equation:

$$\hat{y}_j = \alpha + \beta_1 y_{0,j} + \beta_2 n_j + \beta_3 \sec_j + \beta_4 i_j \tag{2.1}$$

where $\hat{y}_j$ is the growth of per-capita GDP over some period in country j, $y_{0,j}$ is initial per-capita GDP in country j, n_j is population growth over the same period, $\sec_j$ is the secondary school enrollment rate (measured in the beginning period), and i_j is the investment share of GDP over the period.[13] Inclusion of initial per-capita GDP levels (y_0) as an explanatory variable follows from the importance of catch-up in the growth process. Economies can expect rapid growth when they are far behind the leading countries. Secondary school enrollment is included as a proxy for human capital. We discuss the importance of this variable below and in Chapter 5. The key policy variable, however, is the investment rate. Some fixed effect variables might affect growth but are very difficult to change. For example, Russia cannot change its climate.[14] Of all the policy and institutional variables, investment is uniquely important.

Using the Levine–Renelt approach, Fischer and Sahay (2000) confirmed that investment is crucial for growth in transition economies. A further refinement by Crafts and Kaiser (2004) made two important adjustments. First, they used additional explanatory variables such as the rule of law to tighten the forecasts. Second, they adjusted the initial income variable to measure the gap from the frontier at the start of transition, not earlier. Again, investment stood out as the key determinant.

Sutela (2003: 216–17) used the Levine–Renelt approach to explore the prospects for Russian economic growth under three different scenarios for investment: a basic scenario which employs the historical average investment rate of 21 percent, an optimistic scenario which uses 30 percent, and a pessimistic scenario which uses a rate of 15 percent. Sutela showed that the long-run growth rate more than doubles going from the pessimistic to the optimistic scenario.[15] His forecasts for $\hat{y}$ are given in Table 2.1.

Sutela finds that a 10 percentage point increase in the rate of investment leads to a 1.75 percentage point increase in the growth rate of GDP per-capita. To double GDP in a span of ten years would require a growth rate of around 7.2 percent, far higher than in any of Sutela's scenarios. Indeed, if we use his model to calculate the rate of investment required to achieve such growth we understand why he presumably regarded it as too high to be realistic: Russia would have to invest on average no less than 45 percent of its GDP for ten years to double GDP.

Table 2.1 Forecasts for Russian GDP growth using the Levine–Renelt equation (Sutela 2003)

	Investment rate	Per-capita GDP growth (ŷ)
Pessimistic scenario	15%	2.0%
Baseline scenario	21%	3.0%
Optimistic scenario	30%	4.7%

How high is investment in Russia?

The Soviet growth model was extensive, and investment rates exceeded 30 percent (see Ofer 1987: 1786). Much of this investment was wasted, however, owing to the well-known inefficiencies of the Soviet model. Hence, when transition started, there was need for investment to modernize the capital stock even as old capital had to be (or should have been) written off. This suggests two questions: To what extent did Russia invest in the post-Soviet era, and how does this compare to other fast-growing economies?

We can summarize our findings in terms of three comparisons. First, the Russian investment rate is less than those observed in fast-growing ("miracle") economies. Second, Russia's investment rate is less than in EU accession countries. Third, Russian investment rates are only mid-ranking in the pack of CIS countries.

Traditional comparisons

Measured in the traditional manner – ratio of investment to GDP measured at domestic prices – Russia's investment rate is not that high by international standards. Figure 2.1 shows that the investment rate in Russia has been far below historical and current rates in Japan, China, South Korea, and the Czech Republic. Korea's growth take-off occurred when its investment rate rose above 25 percent, with so-called miracle periods occurring when the rate was even higher. Russia, in contrast, saw its investment rate drop to below 20 percent by the mid-1990s and down to under 15 percent in the crisis period of 1998–9. Since then it has recovered – this is the sharp recovery in investment and the rapid growth year to year that is talked about quite often. Nonetheless, it is apparent that this is still significantly lower than other comparable economies.

The low levels of Russian investment are also evident in Table 2.2, which gives the average investment rate over the period 1995–2010 for transition economies. Russia's investment rate is below that of all the EU accession

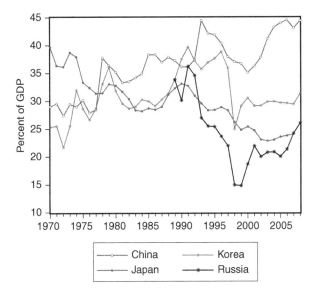

Figure 2.1 Gross capital formation for selected economies, domestic prices

Table 2.2 Investment rates in transition economies (average rates for 1995–2010)

EU accession	Investment/GDP ratio	Ex Soviet Union	Investment/GDP ratio
Slovakia	28.9	Azerbaijan	34.1
Czech Republic	29.1	Belarus	25.4
Hungary	25.8	Ukraine	21.5
Estonia	30.2	Tajikistan	16.5
Slovenia	25.5	Uzbekistan	22.1
Poland	21.4	Russia	20.3
Lithuania	22.0	Kyrgizia	17.7
Latvia	24.7	Armenia	21.3
Romania	21.4	Kazakhstan	22.2
Bulgaria	18.2	Georgia	25.2

Source: World Economic Outlook Database, April 2012.

countries save Bulgaria, and it is also lower than all but two of the post-Soviet countries.

The fact that investment rates in Russia are lower now than in the early 1990s (let alone in the Soviet period) may be less important if there has been a significant increase in the efficiency of investment. After all, one goal of economic reform is to improve the nature of the investment process. Whether efficiency has actually risen is an important question that we discuss below. It is important to note, however, that the investment rate is also low compared not only to fast-growing economies but also to slower-growing ones, too, such as the Czech Republic and Japan in the 1990s.

One obvious and important conclusion is that if Russia did not have oil, this investment rate would have resulted in much slower growth. Russia's GDP level and its growth rate are enhanced by its resource abundance.

Comparisons at international prices

In the previous section we analyzed Russian investment rates measured at domestic prices. Development economists, however, have increasingly turned to measuring investment at international prices, which are more useful for cross-country comparisons because relative prices differ across countries and exchange rates are affected by factors other than national price levels.[16] Using international prices allows one to measure the true value of the physical capital obtained as a result of the investment effort. If the price of investment in a country is high relative to the prices of other components of GDP, this means that the country gets less increase in capital stock per unit of savings than in a country with a lower relative price. De Long and Summers (1991; 1993) stress the distinction

> between investment effort – share of national product saved, plus capital inflows – and investment – buildings constructed and machines put into productive use. Many of the policies that have been followed in the post-World War II period, especially in the developing world, seem designed to maximize "investment effort," while ensuring that each unit of "investment effort" translates into as little actual investment as possible.[17]

This is an important issue for development economists because in many developing economies investment is subject to many policy distortions. The relative price of investment when measured at international prices is on average higher in poor countries than in rich countries.[18] This means that measuring investment rates at international prices will boost the investment share of GDP in richer countries relative to poor countries.[19]

Using international prices, let us return to an examination of the investment rates of the "miracle" economies. A comparison of Figure 2.2 with Figure 2.1 shows that investment rates are lower when measured at international prices, especially for Russia, but this also holds true for China and Japan. The implication is that the relative price of investment is higher for these economies when measured at international prices, so

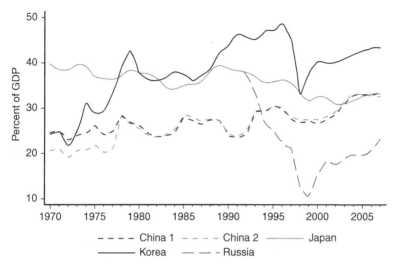

Investment share of PPP converted GDP per capita at current prices

Figure 2.2 Investment rate at international prices for miracle economies and Russia

Source: PWT 6.3.

less actual capital accumulation is obtained from the sacrifice of current consumption.

For transition economies there is an extra complication. Under the Soviet system, planners' preferences ensured that the relative price of investment was low. Consumption was a residual priority. Hence, liberalization of prices caused a shock to the relative price of investment, pushing it up in the early stages of transition.[20] In the ensuing period, however, the relative price of investment declined. Figure 2.3 shows this decline in Hungary and Poland. In Poland the decrease in the relative price of investment was more immediate – a reflection of the quicker pace of price liberalization in general. In both cases, however, the relative price of investment was significantly lower in the second half of the 1990s than in the first half. Hence, transition led to an effectively lower relative price of investment in Hungary and Poland.

In Russia, too, price liberalization led to an upward shock to the relative price of investment. Subsequently, however, the relative price of investment did not decline, as it did in Hungary and Poland, but continued to rise. Indeed, the distortion in relative prices (which could be measured as the difference from unity) has more than doubled during transition. A similar tale can be told for Ukraine.

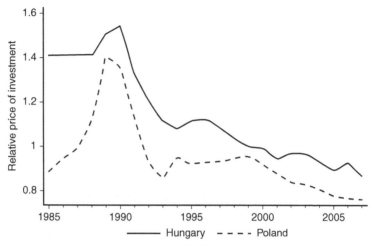

Price of investment relative to the US over price of consumption relative to the US

Figure 2.3 The relative price of investment in Hungary and Poland: the impact of liberalization and transition

Source: PWT 6.3.

Measured at international prices, the relative price of investment is high in transition economies in general, and in Russia in particular (see Figure 2.4). Note that the dispersion in relative prices among those countries has increased over the period, the coefficient of variation rising from 0.188 in 1991 to 0.304 in 2000.[21] This is somewhat surprising. One might expect that market reforms would cause the relative price of investment across countries to converge: at least, this would be so if all differences in relative prices were due to distortions caused by central planning. These are important, but they are not the only distortionary factors. For example, governments in market economies may engage in policies that distort prices. The evidence presented in Figure 2.4 suggests that this is what is taking place in Russia and especially in Ukraine.

Given the high relative price of investment in Russia (and Ukraine), it follows that investment rates are lower when measured at international prices (Figure 2.5). The adjustment is quite dramatic for Russia. Table 2.2 showed that Russia invested, on average, about 20 percent of GDP at domestic prices over the period 1995–2010. At international prices, however, its investment rate fell below 10 percent after 1998. Adjustment for international prices reduces investment rates for all of the economies displayed in Figure 2.5, but the adjustment is highest for Russia and Ukraine. Moreover, the gap between those two and the rest increased during the second half of the 1990s.

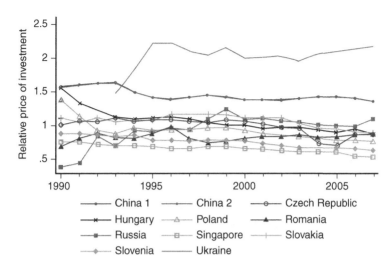

Figure 2.4 The relative price of investment in transition economies

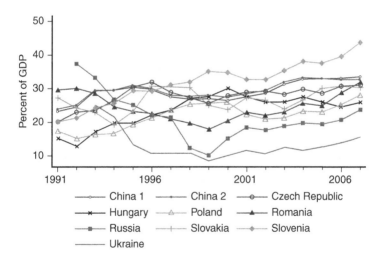

Figure 2.5 Gross capital formation at international prices, transition economies

Growth equations revisited

If measuring investment at international prices produces such a different picture, it begs the question: How does it affect projections of growth? To answer this we return to the Levine–Renelt equations, but now we use investment at international prices in the model. We estimate the equation using data from 1960–89 for the same countries to maintain comparability with Levine–Renelt, although we can also extend the data period (and do so below). In addition, we also treat the education variable differently. Levine–Renelt used the level of secondary school *enrollment* as of the beginning period, 1960. We instead use the share of the population aged 15 and over that has *attained at least* the level of secondary school (BLSECA) as of 1960.[22] Human capital is a stock, so the attainment variable seems more in accord with what we want to measure than the enrollment level. We also include a squared term for educational attainment (BLSECASQ) to account for the non-linear impact of education levels on growth. The reason we want to consider this non-linearity is that when educational attainment is already at high levels, as it is in Russia, then the marginal gain from increased attainment might be very different than in the average country.

Table 2.3 presents the coefficients obtained from the Levine–Renelt equation and from our alternative. It should not be surprising that the results for several of the variables on the two equations are quite similar. The effects of initial income (Y60) and population growth over the period (DPOP) are essentially the same in both equations. It is interesting to compare the educational variables in the two equations, since in our analysis we suggest the effect of education may be non-linear. In fact, the squared-term (BLSECASQ) is statistically significant and the coefficient is negative. This implies that as a country educates more and more of its population, the marginal impact on growth of increases in attainment rapidly diminishes. This is important for our analysis because in the Barro–Lee attainment data Russia has among the highest levels of educational attainment.

Our real focus, of course, is the coefficient for investment. That figure is considerably lower in our preferred alternative – 12.5 as compared with Levine–Renelt's 17.5. By measuring investment shares at international prices (the PPP measure) we are gauging the impact of *actual investment*, rather than *investment effort*, as in the Levine–Renelt equation. Actual investment during this period was less than investment effort, so the Levine–Renelt equation assigns more impact to investment than is warranted. Russia achieved less growth as a direct result of its savings than appears to be the case when using investment at domestic prices.

Table 2.3 Growth equations compared

Variable	Levine–Renelt	Gaddy–Ickes
Constant	−0.83	0.87
	(0.97)	(1.20)
Y60	−0.35	−0.27
	(2.50)	(3.85)
DPOP	−0.38	−0.41
	(1.73)	(1.97)
SEC	3.17	
	(2.46)	
BLSECA		7.83
		(2.65)
BLSECASQ		−8.05
		(1.99)
Investment	17.5	12.52
	(6.53)	(6.13)
R^2	0.46	0.48
N	101	91

Note: *t*-statistics in parentheses, White corrected standard errors.

Using our estimates from Table 2.3 and Russia's initial conditions as of 2004, we can revisit the issue of doubling Russia's GDP in ten years. Our idea is to use our preferred alternative to the original Levine–Renelt model, that is, using an investment variable measured at international prices and a modified education variable. Of the explanatory variables in the model, the only real policy instrument is the investment rate, so we plug in the actual values of the other variables and ask what rate of investment is needed to obtain a growth rate that will double GDP in ten years. Recall that Sutela's (2003) findings implied that an investment rate of 45 percent would be required to double Russia's GDP in ten years. Since the coefficient on investment that we obtained is lower, we know that the investment rate will have to be even higher. In fact, our model implies that the investment rate would have to be over 56 percent of GDP to achieve Putin's goal.

There are two important points to make about this result. Such a sacrifice of current consumption for future growth would exceed even the accumulation rates of the Soviet period,[23] or those of the "miracle growth" experiences in Figure 2.1 (aside from China). The reason that countries do not have such high savings rates is because the sacrifice is too great – that is, the rewards are not worth it. Moreover, even if such high savings rates were to be achieved, it would be incredible if sufficient investments could be made without a sharp deterioration of the effectiveness of investment. A very rapid investment rate would likely result in an increase in the relative price of capital and less bang for the investment buck. But the doubling of

GDP based on a 56 percent investment rate is based on the presumption that the marginal efficiency of investment would not change.[24] Obviously, if this presumption failed, an even higher rate of investment would be needed!

The fact that Russia has grown rapidly over the past decade without such fantastic investment rates is testimony to how important Russia's oil has been for its growth. It also suggests that because Russia does have oil, it does not need to invest 56 percent of GDP in order to grow at satisfactory rates. But this also points out how misguided is the idea that Russia should diversify out of oil. There are two reasons for this. First, and most directly, the increase in oil wealth, thanks mainly to price increases, is the primary generator of Russian growth. Second, the abundance of oil has raised the relative price of investment compared with that of countries without oil. The implications of this second point are critical. Because of Russia's high relative price of investment, diversification into manufacturing is likely to result in much less growth than would be the case in a less resource-abundant economy.

Why is the relative price of investment so high in Russia?

The high relative price of investment in Russia is, in fact, a manifestation of the Soviet inheritance in all its forms: a legacy of state-owned enterprises, mis-location, and, most importantly, resource addiction.[25] Schmitz (2001) studied the impact of production of investment goods by government-owned enterprises in Egypt and Turkey and showed that the impact on aggregate productivity could be quite large. Assuming that state-owned capital goods producers are 50 percent as productive as privately-owned producers (the result based on case studies in these countries), aggregate productivity is only 64 percent of its potential level. Of course, in the case of Russia all investment goods producers were 100 percent state owned prior to privatization, and little restructuring seems to have taken place in many of these enterprises (see, for example, Palmeda and Lewis 2001).

A common cross-country observation is that the relative price of investment goods is higher in poorer countries. Hsieh and Klenow (2007) show that this is because of higher relative productivity in consumer goods industries in poorer countries. This seems also to be the case in Russia, although perhaps for different reasons. In the Soviet period consumer goods industries were low-prestige industries and suffered from underinvestment. The relative low political weight of consumer goods industries probably also means that these sectors found it harder to resist entry. In the post-Soviet period they have received the overwhelming bulk of non-oil foreign direct investment (FDI). This presumably promotes productivity growth in consumption goods industries.

In Table 2.4 we present calculations of the relative price of investment (measured as the ratio of the price of investment goods to the price of

Table 2.4 Investment price ratios by type

	USA	Hungary	Poland	Russia	Singapore	Czech Republic	Ukraine
Construction	1.15	1.24	1.23	1.86	1.68	1.17	2.28
Machinery and equipment	0.95	2.06	1.94	2.74	0.65	2.52	5.33
Stocks	1.06	1.68	2.03	2.31	1.43	2.05	3.13
All capital formation	1.05	1.55	1.54	2.12	0.89	1.72	2.95

Note: Ratios shown are the prices of investment goods of each type relative to consumption goods.
Source: Penn World Tables, 6.3 and authors' calculations. Data are for 1996.

consumption goods, P_I/P_C), for capital formation as a whole and by type of investment. The high relative price of investment for Russia stands out (2.12 compared with 1.05 in the US). Even in other transition countries, aside from Ukraine, it is lower. What is even more important, however, is the very high relative price for machinery and equipment. For, as we discuss below in the section on the τ effect, machinery and equipment is the most important component of capital formation for enhancing productivity growth.

A key legacy of the Soviet period was the collection of low productivity assets. According to one estimate, these were 30 percent as productive as US assets in 1992 (Palmeda and Lewis 2001: 48), although any such calculations are difficult to assess. Many dinosaur enterprises managed to survive the upheaval at the end of the Soviet period; they did not go extinct. This was accomplished by resorting to survival strategies that exploited non-economic instruments.[26] The Soviet legacy in relation to capital was one of hypertrophied machine building and defense enterprises. This was a direct result of the militarization of the Soviet economy. There was a distinct dual use imperative in the Soviet economy (Gaddy 1996), and this lowered productivity. These problems should become less important through the passage of time: as capital depreciates, new enterprises built in the market economy should replace dinosaur enterprises. Russia's problem – its potential bear trap – is that rent addiction serves to sustain the dinosaurs.[27] In a way Russia shares this problem with any country with a history of inward-oriented development. De Long and Summers (1993: 399) write:

[In] India, like in Argentina, the savings rate is relatively high but equipment is expensive .... India demonstrates not that boosting investment is unproductive, but that policies that boost saving while simultaneously raising the relative price of investment in equipment and structures are unproductive. We suspect that restrictions on imports of capital goods have ensured that the Indian government's attempts to support investment have had effects not on quantities but on prices: India's policies have managed to enrich *industrialists* instead of encouraging *industry*.

But in Russia inward-oriented development was taken to an extreme not witnessed anywhere else. In the Russian case, the contrast is perhaps that attempts to support investment have ensured the survival of dinosaurs at the expense of encouraging industry.[28]

The preservation of dinosaurs and the inward orientation have important productivity effects. As Jones (2011) emphasizes, inefficiency in intermediate goods production has a multiplier effect on productivity differences across countries. The reason is that low productivity in intermediate goods production is passed through the economy along chains of production.[29] Jones (2011: 2) notes:

> Low productivity in electric power generation – for example, because of theft, inferior technology, or misallocation – makes electricity more costly, which reduces output in banking and construction. But this in turn makes it harder to finance and build new dams and therefore further hinders electric power generation.

Inefficiency at each link in the chain of intermediate production leads to higher prices for final goods production. If these inefficiencies in the production process are prevalent in the capital goods sector – where the dinosaurs still reside – then the relative price of investment will be raised further.[30]

Consequences of the high relative price of investment

The consequences of the high relative price of investment in Russia are several. First, growth is lower than would be expected given Russia's savings rate. For any level of savings, the addition to the capital stock is lower. Russia obtains a lower return than would be expected from its sacrifice owing to the "tax" it pays on investment. Hence, when we compare the relative price of investment with growth performance, it is not surprising that we find a strong negative relationship for transition economies, as in Figure 2.6. In the case of Russia this effect is masked, to a large degree, by the country's resource abundance, which fuels growth independently.

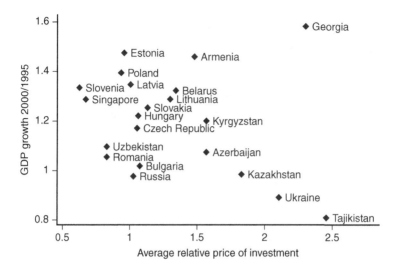

Figure 2.6 Relative price of investment and GDP growth, selected countries
Source: PWT 6.3.

Second, the high relative price of investment and, consequently, the lower level of actual investment (as opposed to investment effort) means that the goal of diversifying the Russian economy out of oil and raw materials is more distant than thought.

Geography and capital

In addition to the issue of mismeasurement of the relative price of investment, there is another important way in which Russia's investment figures are inflated. It is a problem for which there is unfortunately no remedy. National income accounting is confronted with a dilemma when it comes to investment made for the purpose of adjusting to climate, distance, and other aspects of geographical terrain. Kravis *et al.* (1982: 28) identify the general problem as follows:

> Suppose that in a cold climate a steam power plant had to be built with insulating walls around its boiler room and switchhouse, whereas in a warm climate both can be exposed to the weather. Assuming that all other characteristics are identical, should the inputs and costs required for closed construction in the cold climate be regarded simply as added costs, or as more output?

Their conclusion is that such investment should be counted as extra costs. In practice, however, that is not done. On the contrary, the standard in national income accounting is to count such investment as added output. They explain (1982: 28–9):

> The cost of a flat road of a given specification in one country was compared with the cost of a road of the same specification in another country, and likewise for a mountainous road. The effect, of course, was to treat the mountainous road as more output than a flat road; in a sense, an adverse environment in this instance required more production, just as low temperatures necessitated the provision of heat and warm clothing. Similarly, insulating walls for power plants in cold climates were regarded as part of output rather than mere addition to cost.[31]

To repeat: all extra investment in any country that is made to compensate for "adverse environment" is considered statistically as an addition to capital. This means that even though a power plant built in Siberia, say, requires extra heating and insulation compared with one in Mexico, that greater cost is not counted as an expense but as output. Consequently, it shows up as greater investment. For most countries of the world such cases are exceptional and probably have no significant effect on measurement of total investment. But, while this phenomenon may be no more than statistical noise for other countries, it is highly important for Russia, the world's largest and coldest country. In the next chapter we will deal more thoroughly with the questions of cold and distance. Suffice it to state here that if one were able to account for the portion of capital accumulation that goes to compensate for Russia's geography, investment would be relatively even more expensive, especially as this applies most to structures, and we have seen that the composition of Russian investment is skewed in that direction.

The τ effect

What Kravis *et al.* are saying is that capital can be handicapped by location. It may be in extremely remote locations, cold locations, mountainous regions, and so forth. One way to think of such handicapped capital – capital in what Kravis *et al.* refer to as an adverse environment – is that in each period more capital depreciates than would otherwise be the case. Hence, a greater portion of gross investment is really replacement, although this extra replacement is made not in order to compensate for wear and tear or even for economic obsolescence but rather to allow capital to function as it would in a normal environment. Failure (or inability) to account for this depreciation results in overmeasurement of the capital stock. If, as we have shown in the previous sections, this is a problem that afflicts Russia in particular, it is important to develop an approach that can recognize the effect of that mismeasurement. We suggest such an approach below.

Suppose that we can index by τ the ratio of the true capital stock to the measured capital stock (τ is thus a mismeasurement index). Now consider the return to capital. The actual return to capital will differ from the return to measured capital. So if the production function is of the customary Cobb–Douglas form, we should write

$$Y_i = \tau K_i^\alpha \, (A_i L_i)^{1-\alpha} \tag{2.2}$$

where Y denotes output, K is capital, L is labor in efficiency units, and A is total factor productivity. If τ is ignored, the marginal product of capital appears as $\alpha K_i^{\alpha-1} (A_i L_i)^{1-\alpha}$. But if one does recognize τ the actual marginal product of capital is $\alpha\tau K_i^{\alpha-1}(A_i L_i)^{1-\alpha}$. And if $\tau < 1$ it is obvious that

$$\alpha K_i^{\alpha-1} (A_i L_i)^{1-\alpha} > \alpha\tau K_i^{\alpha-1}(A_i L_i)^{1-\alpha}$$

In other words, the measured marginal product of capital is in fact larger than the actual marginal product of capital. This means that the impact of investment is overstated if measured capital is inflated. Alternatively, the difference in income levels – as in development accounting – overstates the impact of differences in A's, as it understates differences in functioning capital stocks across countries. This diverts attention from problems with factor accumulation and towards efficiency considerations.[32] This is not to say that the efficiency problems are unimportant, but ignoring systematic mismeasurement problems results in a lack of attention paid to differences in capital stocks.

As the citations from Kravis *et al.* indicate, all countries may have instances of inflated capital. But in the case of Russia, which is both the largest country in terms of territory and the coldest in terms of temperature, this phenomenon is systematic, not random. So ignoring $\tau < 1$ is likely to be much more problematic in the case of Russia than in almost any other country in the world. This has important implications for thinking about Russia's relative inability to attract FDI. Conventional wisdom is that barriers, restrictions, and taxes on investment are the chief culprits in preventing capital flows to developing economies. So, the argument goes, if these restrictions are removed, FDI will flow to Russia. But if $\tau < 1$, rates of return may be insufficient to attract investment even if the "chief culprit" is eliminated. Because if $\tau < 1$ is due to geographic burdens, as it is in Russia, then removing the institutional barriers will not solve the problem. Such reforms will not make Russia more compact or warmer.

All countries (except, perhaps, Singapore, where $\tau = 1$ – the country is a city, after all) have a $\tau < 1$. But the handicaps that any country faces can be decomposed into self-imposed part and a fixed effect. The latter is due to irreducible features of the environment to which the country has optimally adapted. The former refers to the extra costs imposed by misallocation. The approach of Kravis *et al.* is to acknowledge $\tau < 1$ but treat it as measurement error. Their implicit assumption is that differences in τ across countries are not systematic and thus can be ignored in comparative analysis. This may be true in general, but if one were to take their discussion seriously one would realize that the data for some countries, notably Russia, would have systematic biases.

Machinery and equipment

DeLong and Summers (1993) argue that machinery and equipment is the most important component of capital accumulation in explaining productivity growth.[33] Ideas may be embodied in capital goods, and it is in machinery and equipment that this embodiment takes place. Employing modern machinery and equipment requires skills that are important for growth. Moreover, as it is investment in equipment, not structures, that is associated with growth, it is much more likely that the former causes the latter than an instance of reverse causation.[34] They were also able to show that the effect applies to developing countries; it is not just a rich country effect.

The argument that machinery and equipment is the essential feature of capital accumulation is even more important when we think about Russia. Much capital accumulation in Russia goes towards coping with location and size, such as transportation investment and insulation, neither of which brings new ideas or increases total factor productivity. In Russia a large portion of transportation falls into the same category as insulation in Siberia, that is, it should properly be regarded as an extra cost rather than as investment.[35] Capital formation in Russia consists to a much greater extent than in the US, say, of construction as opposed to producer durables. Whereas in the US about 50 percent of capital accumulation goes to machinery and equipment, in Russia it is less than a quarter (see the column "Share of producer durables" in Table 2.5). Moreover, construction is the type of capital formation that lends itself most to corruption in all countries.[36] And, of course, corruption is high in all the post-Soviet countries. Given that the relative price of machinery and equipment investment is high in Russia, it is not surprising that the share of capital accumulation that takes this form is comparatively low.

Table 2.5 Components of domestic capital formation

	Share of construction	Share of producer durables	Share of changes in stocks
Belarus	0.82	0.13	0.60
Brazil	0.69	0.31	0.0
Czech Republic	0.57	0.36	0.06
Germany	0.54	0.44	0.03
Hungary	0.53	0.28	0.19
Romania	0.59	0.34	0.07
Russia	0.62	0.22	0.15
Singapore	0.25	0.77	–0.02
Slovakia	0.66	0.30	0.03
Ukraine	0.73	0.20	0.08
United States	0.48	0.50	0.02

Source: Penn World Tables, 6.3. Data are for 1996.

Conclusion

In our simple exercise to determine the investment rate needed to double GDP, we used PPP investment rates (investment at international prices). This produced the estimate that the investment share of GDP would have to rise to 56 percent in order to double Russian GDP in ten years. However, this is not the end of the story. Even the PPP measures, it turns out, overvalue investment in Russia. This is because space and cold issues are not taken into account in the data on GDP and its components using international prices – for fundamental reasons. Russia gets even less per unit of effort than other countries would, so the amount of sacrificed consumption Russia would require to grow at acceptable rates without oil is immense. There are two aspects of this problem to consider. First, since Russia is colder on average than other countries, it spends more investment effort on insulation and in overcoming other geographic hurdles than other countries do. So, comparatively, its relative price of capital is even higher than measured. Second, Russia has located too much economic activity in places that have geographic handicaps, so this reinforces the problem. The first problem cannot be overcome, and thus some mismeasurement relative to other countries is inevitable, but the second could be addressed by overturning the legacies of past location decisions. That is, if the second problem were addressed, the consequences of the first problem would be less severe.

The analysis clearly implies that Russia gets credit for investment that should not be counted. Statistically, it gets rewarded rather than penalized for bad location decisions. To achieve the same flow of capital services a plant in Novosibirsk requires more investment than one in Moscow, but this extra investment is compensation for cold and distance; it adds nothing to productivity. Hence, poor location decisions make Russia's capital stock look larger than it really is: it makes τ_K even smaller. But productivity is still low.[37] This problem is not just about the initial investment decision. All further investment to maintain that location is similarly mismeasured. While we cannot adjust statistics for this, this problem is likely to be very significant. In the next chapter we examine the hurdles posed by location legacies.

3 The economics of location

Introduction

In Chapter 2 we noted how Russia's physical capital stock is mismeasured (overstated) owing to the failure to account for space and cold. We noted how a cold climate may require extra insulation for factories; building a road across mountainous terrain requires additional costs. These extra expenditures should properly be treated as costs and be deducted from investment to obtain an economically appropriate measure of the capital stock. Because these costs are hidden, they can be a bear trap. That is, investment in human capital or physical capital that is designed to enhance growth may have negative effects unless that investment is made with full appreciation of the effect of location. This chapter will analyze the excess costs of faulty location decisions. The next chapter will focus on why these extra costs persist.

From the point of view of economic efficiency, the dominant characteristic of the Soviet period was misallocation. The country's resources (including human resources) were misused. The Soviet system produced the wrong things. Its factories produced them in the wrong way. It educated its people with the wrong skills. But perhaps worst of all, communist planners put factories, machines, and people in the wrong places. For a country with so much territory, especially territory in remote and cold places, location matters a great deal. Not only did Russia suffer from the irrationality of central planning for more than 70 years, but Russia's vast territorial expanse offered latitude for that system to make mistakes of spatial allocation on a huge and unprecedented scale. Had the Bolshevik Revolution taken place instead in a country as small and contained as, say, Japan, the damage would not have been as great.[1] While central planning would still have distorted the economy, it would not, and could not, have distorted it as much in terms of locational decisions. The sheer magnitude of these locational errors would have been much less and would have been a much smaller handicap to this hypothetical "transitional Japanese economy." In Russia, Siberia gave central planners great room for error, and unfortunately this opportunity was exploited to the fullest.[2] Failure to recognize this legacy of Soviet planning is one of the most important bear traps we analyze in this book.

In this chapter we consider two types of costs associated with spatial misallocation: cold and distance. Both are critically important in the Russian context. Estimating the costs of misallocation in "thermal space" – that is, building factories and cities in unnecessarily cold locations – is, as we will show, a complex question. Still, there are methods that can yield useful estimates. The issue of distance or remoteness costs is less tractable. The methods we use for thermal misallocation fail when we attempt to apply them to the problem of distance. What we can do is outline the nature of the problem of economic distance. We discuss the reasons for the difference between cold and space and conclude by explaining the features of the bear trap generated by cold and distance.

Thermal misallocation: the cost of the cold[3]

We begin by focusing on thermal misallocation – the cost of the cold. Not only does Russia's uniquely large land mass lie in an extreme high-latitude (northern) position but very little of that territory enjoys any moderating influence of temperate oceans in the east and west. It has twice as much territory above the Arctic Circle as Canada, ten times as much as Alaska, and fifteen times as much as Norway, Sweden, and Finland combined.

Locations in the heart of eastern Russia are frequently the coldest spots on the globe on a day-to-day basis. In fact, the lowest temperature ever recorded outside Antarctica, –68 °C, was in Russia.[4] But, of course, much more meaningful for the economist than the temperatures of remote locations are those in major population centers. A comparison of Russian cities with counterparts in Canada and the United States is instructive. Of the 100 coldest (measured by the average January temperature) Russian and North American cities with populations of over 100,000, Russia has 85, Canada 10, and the United States 5. Ranked in order of cold, the first Canadian city to appear on the list (Winnipeg) is in 22nd place. The coldest US city (Fargo, North Dakota) ranks 58th. Surprising to some, perhaps, no Alaskan city even appears on the list – not because Alaska is not cold but because Americans do not build large cities in Alaska. Anchorage is the only city in Alaska with a population of over 100,000, but it is not cold enough to make the top 100. For very large cities, the comparison is even more skewed to Russia. The United States, for instance, has only one metropolitan area with a population of over half a million (Minneapolis-St. Paul) that has a mean January temperature colder than –8 °C. Russia has 30 cities that big and that cold.

Duluth and Perm

The two cities of Duluth, Minnesota, and Perm, Russia, and their evolution in the twentieth century provide an instructive comparison of urban growth in cold climates. These two cities are quite similar in terms of climate, location, and their size around the year 1900. Perm's mean January temperature is about one degree colder than Duluth's. Both cities are relatively far from large markets but close to abundant resource bases. At the start of the twentieth century Duluth (population just above 50,000) was a little larger than Perm (just below 50,000).

In the first few decades of the century Duluth grew rapidly. By 1930 the population of the city had reached 101,000 and that of the greater metropolitan area (the metropolitan statistical area, or MSA) was 211,000. This was fueled by the establishment of a large US Steel plant in 1915, ostensibly to take advantage of its proximity to iron ore and Lake Superior.[5] Predictions that Duluth would rival Pittsburgh or Detroit were heard. Yet, population growth ceased around this time and, today, Duluth has a population of approximately 86,000. What happened?

The fate of the Minnesota Steel Company illustrates the difficulties Duluth faced in becoming an industrial powerhouse.[6] Its location offered favorable access to iron ore and cheap transportation for other key inputs such as coal and limestone. But the cold raised the cost of production. Temperatures that could frequently reach –22 °C in January meant that equipment required extra insulation and other special modifications to avoid frequently breaking down. The cold also raised the cost of living in Duluth, and this added to labor costs. The biggest handicap, however, was (a lack of) proximity to markets. This more than offset the advantage of the local resource base. As White and Primmer (1937: 90–91) noted:

> The successful location of iron and steel plants is largely a matter of transportation costs, but not, as is so commonly assumed, of freight charges on raw materials only. Transportation charges on finished steel to the point of consumption are equally, if not even more, significant. It is here that Duluth's weakness … become(s) apparent: Duluth, situated in a region where farming is the chief occupation, obviously requires little steel …. The selection of the head of Lake Superior as a site for iron and steel-manufacture thus appears to be a striking example of locational maladjustment.

Duluth was too cold and too far from its principal markets to make it as an industrial center. Market forces worked: Duluth ceased to grow as an industrial center and its population stagnated.

In the 1930s Perm experienced even more rapid growth than Duluth. From a population of 67,000 in 1923 (Russia's 31st largest city), Perm tripled in size by 1939 to become the 13th largest in Russia. Unlike that of Duluth, Perm's growth was not the result of a desire to exploit local resources.[7] Rather, it was primarily fueled by the defense industry. Twelve giant plants (over 10,000 workers each) were built in Perm in three distinct phases from the 1930s to the 1960s (Gaddy 1996: figure 9.1, 160–61).

Perm is as cold and remote as Duluth. It has even more extremely cold days on average, and it is similarly far from markets. But because of central planning these factors did not inhibit its growth. Perm did not stop growing until the 1980s, when its population exceeded a million. Today, it is still larger than the entire Duluth-Superior, Wisconsin, metropolitan area by a factor of four. Because market signals were irrelevant to the growth of Perm until the end of the Soviet era, the "maladjustment" process could continue for much longer. In Duluth market feedback limited the damage.[8]

Measuring cold: temperature per-capita

For some, Russia's problem with the cold is God-given and fixed.[9] This ignores the extent to which thermal misallocation (like other aspects of spatial misallocation) is the result of past decisions. What matters economically is not the temperature of Russia's land mass *per se* but where economic activity is conducted in that space. The central point is that population distribution, and hence a country's temperature in an economic sense, is the result of human choices. Russia's climate would be colder than Spain's regardless of the decisions of central planners. But that does not mean that Russia's central planners could not make things worse. They did, and it is important to see by how much. This gives us some idea of the excess cold Russia suffers. That is, how much was the unavoidable result of Russia's geography and how much is due to allocative mistakes of the past?

Studies of the effects of temperature on economic activity have typically used some variant of an average national temperature that is the mean of recorded temperatures spaced fairly evenly across the country. What is important for our purposes is the temperature of places where people actually live and work. If we look only at territorial temperature averages, then the countries of northern Europe – Sweden, Norway, and Finland – appear to be cold. In fact, in these countries the population is concentrated along the coasts and in the south, where temperatures are not significantly different from the rest of Europe. The same is true for Canada, where most people live along the southern border.

The "Cost of the Cold" project (described in note 3) introduced the concept of temperature per-capita (TPC) – a population-weighted mean temperature. We define the TPC of country k as:

$$TPC_k = \sum_j n_j t_j \tag{3.1}$$

where n_j is the share of a country's total population that resides in region j, and t_j is the mean temperature in region j. In our work on the cold, we measure TPC for the month of January over an extended historical period.

TPC can be used for both cross-country and time-series comparisons. Canada's territory, for instance, lies in a northerly range that is similar to Russia's. But Canada's population distribution is very different, with a much larger proportion of the total population living in the southernmost part of the country. Is Russia then colder than Canada? For that matter, is Russia colder than other northern countries, such as Sweden? And how might the countries have changed over time owing to population movement? If a country's territory offers a range of temperature zones, its TPC could theoretically rise or fall if people moved to warmer or colder regions.

Table 3.1 compares Russia with other cold-climate countries in around 1930, before the most serious misallocation in Russia under central economic planning had occurred. At that point, Russia was already "economically colder" than not only the United States but also Sweden and Canada – more than 1.5 °C colder than Canada and well over 7 °C colder than Sweden.

What is noteworthy is the contrast between Russia and the other countries in the subsequent period. Figure 3.1 shows that Russia became even colder during the rest of the twentieth century, ending up a full degree colder by 1989. Meanwhile, Canada's TPC rose by more than one degree in the same period, primarily as a result of population moving to the south. In Russia, thanks to Soviet policies that moved population to the extremely cold regions of the east, TPC decreased.

Table 3.1 TPCs of the United States, Sweden, Canada, and Russia around 1930

Country and year	TPC (°C)
USA 1930	1.1
Sweden 1930	−3.9
Canada 1931	−9.9
Russia 1926	−11.6

Note: Authors' calculations.

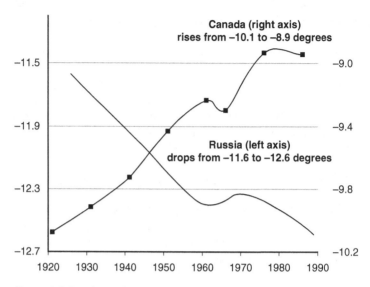

Figure 3.1 Russian and Canadian TPC in the twentieth century

TPC can also be used to identify which specific regions of a country are most responsible for its overall temperature. A very cold place inhabited by only a small number of people may be less important in generating the country's overall TPC than a somewhat warmer (but still cold) location with a large number of people. Table 3.2 shows those Russian cities which, by virtue of their combination of size and cold, contribute most to lowering Russia's national TPC below a benchmark of −10 °C (the January temperature in Moscow).

Clearly, no single city is the whole problem – even the biggest negative contributors, Novosibirsk and Omsk, together account for less than 9 percent of this reduction of TPC below −10 °C. However, as a group these cities are quite significant. To put their importance in perspective, note that there is a total of nearly 1,300 cities with populations of over 10,000 in Russia, home to almost 100 million people. What Table 3.2 implies is that of all these urban areas, the 23 listed account for *nearly half* of the drop in the entire country's TPC below −10 °C.

It is also interesting to note the diversity of the list in terms of the range of both temperature and population. Since the product of temperature and population is the significant factor, the cities fall into three broad categories: (1) relatively small but extremely cold cities (Yakutsk, Ulan-Ude, Norilsk, Chita); (2) very large, although not terribly cold – for Russia – cities (the Urals and Volga valley cities of Yekaterinburg, Chelyabinsk, Perm,

Table 3.2 Leading negative contributors to Russian TPC

City	Location	2010 population (000s)	January temperature (°C)	Percent of cold
Novosibirsk	Siberia	1,474	−19	4.9%
Omsk	Siberia	1,154	−19	3.8%
Yakutsk	Siberia	270	−43	3.4%
Yekaterinburg	Urals	1,350	−16	2.9%
Khabarovsk	Far East	578	−22	2.6%
Ulan-Ude	Siberia	404	−27	2.6%
Krasnoyarsk	Siberia	974	−17	2.5%
Irkutsk	Siberia	587	−21	2.4%
Norilsk	Siberia	175	−35	2.3%
Chita	Siberia	324	−27	2.1%
Chelyabinsk	Urals	1,130	−15	2.0%
Barnaul	Siberia	612	−18	1.8%
Perm	Urals	992	−15	1.8%
Tomsk	Siberia	523	−19	1.7%
Samara	Volga	1,165	−14	1.6%
Novokuznetsk	Siberia	548	−18	1.6%
Kemerovo	Siberia	533	−18	1.6%
Ufa	Volga	1,062	−14	1.5%
Komsomolsk	Far East	264	−24	1.4%
Kazan	Volga	1,144	−13	1.3%
Tyumen	Siberia	582	−16	1.3%
Bratsk	Siberia	246	−23	1.2%
Blagoveshchensk	Far East	214	−24	1.1%

Samara, Ufa); and (3) cold and large cities (the two big Siberian capitals of Novosibirsk and Omsk).

Calculating the cost of the cold

How can we calculate the cost of the cold? Our goal is to estimate the extra cost associated with the location decisions made during the Soviet period. Two steps are required. First, we have to calculate the additional costs incurred as the temperature falls – that is, the direct cost of cold. Second, we have to know how much colder Russia ended up as a result of Soviet policies. Putting the two together allows one to measure the excess cost of the cold. The first part of the exercise employs a "building block" approach. That is, we identify the categories of extra costs per unit of extra cold, and sum them up. For the second part of the exercise we have to compare Russia's actual population distribution with a prediction of what would have happened without central planning: that is, we compare the actual with a counterfactual spatial allocation of the economy under market economy conditions. We discuss the two steps in turn.

To date, no one has conducted the kind of comprehensive research that could say what the total effects of cold are on any economy, much less for Russia specifically. But two strands of research offer partial answers. One is cold engineering, which looks primarily at direct costs. These are the costs that come from reduced work efficiency of both humans and machines, and from damage to buildings, equipment, infrastructure, agriculture, fishing, and human beings (including deaths). The other is the research on the effects of global climate change, which looks also at adaptation costs. Adaptation costs include expenditures of energy for heating, extra materials (and special materials) that are used in the construction of buildings, and infrastructure – in general, all the money and effort that goes into protecting or at least buffering society from the cold.

Cold-region engineering research

Cold-region engineering research studies the effects of variation in temperature on the performance of specific activities, such as mineral extraction, construction, and military activity. These detailed studies focus on performance of tasks and thus place less emphasis on cost than on pure engineering requirements. Nevertheless, the research is valuable because it indicates the degree to which performance deteriorates at cold temperatures and provides evidence of the negative productivity effects of cold temperature.

One of the most useful of these studies for our purposes is that by Abele (1986), which synthesized data from various surveys of the construction industry and the military and illustrates the effect of cold weather on the productivity of people and machines. Figure 3.2 shows the drop in efficiency for manual and equipment tasks involved in typical construction or repair work as the air temperature drops from below freezing to –30 or –40 °C. Below –40 °C any manual work becomes nearly impossible, and even construction equipment is rarely used.

To express how the reduced efficiency translates into increased work effort (in terms of time) required to perform construction or repair work in cold weather, Abele introduced a "cold environment factor" (F) to measure the effort required to perform a task as temperature varies. Thus, at normal temperatures (around +10 to +15 °C for manual tasks and above +5 °C for equipment tasks, with no wind or precipitation), $F = 1$. The cold environment factor rises as adverse weather affects work efficiency. Figure 3.3 shows this relationship for manual (F_m) and equipment tasks (F_e). For instance, at –25 °C the standard time for each manual task would have

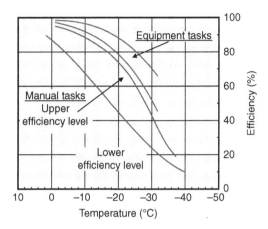

Figure 3.2 The effect of temperature on manual and equipment tasks

Source: Abele (1986).

to be multiplied by 1.6, and the time for each equipment task by about 1.3. At –30 °C these ratios rise to over 2.1 (manual) and 1.6 (equipment), and so on. Perhaps the most important point to note is that the relationship is non-linear. The marginal impact of a fall in temperature on F increases as the temperature falls, so for very cold regions the impact is even greater.

Figure 3.3 shows reduced efficiency due solely to temperature and disregards the effects of other climatic conditions, such as wind and snow.

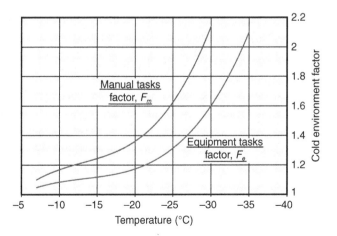

Figure 3.3 Cold environment factors at various temperatures

Source: Abele (1986).

Wind, in particular, is a serious complicating factor for manual tasks in cold weather. The severity of the wind chill effect, relative to the pure temperature effect, can be seen by noting that even at –15 °C a 20 mph (32 kph) wind will produce a manual cold environment factor in excess of 4.0 – in other words, quadrupling task performance times.[10]

The cold regions engineering literature presents a picture of an economic environment that is costly, dangerous, and unpredictable. Cold alters the properties of materials, leading to more accidents and breakdowns, and it reduces the ability of human beings to work efficiently and safely. Unless precautions are taken, serious damage to property and loss of life may result. Many of the studies raise the question of whether it makes economic sense to continue work in these regions, especially during winter months. Engineering studies alone, however, cannot answer this question. What is needed is information about the costs associated with living and building in cold climates. To find such cost estimates, we turn to studies spurred by concern over climate change.

Adaptation to cold: the case of Canada and the US

Reflecting a general concern over the consequences of global climate change, Canadian government agencies in the 1990s attempted to estimate the costs that Canadians incur in adapting to their climate. The problem, researchers found, was that although adaptation does occur, it is rarely accounted for and sometimes barely recognized as having taken place. As they wrote:

> Adaptation to present day climate is the result of a slow accumulation of policies and practices that protect people and property and allow economic and social activities to continue with a minimum of loss or disruption. Adaptation costs are thus "built-in" to routine expenditures and budgets ... Because Canada is a modern industrialized country, it has sophisticated systems which enable Canadians to continue their activities in all but the most extreme weather conditions. Most Canadians take these systems for granted, and indeed believe that the Canadian climate does not much affect them (aside from providing a perennial topic of conversation!). In fact, these systems are so taken for granted that their effectiveness and desirability are seldom evaluated.

To begin to fill in the gaps, the researchers focused on the sectors of the economy most susceptible to climate effects: transportation, construction, agriculture, forestry, water supply and use, household expenditures, emergency planning, and weather forecasting. (They subsumed energy costs under the appropriate sectors.) They then calculated total annual public expenditures for these categories. Table 3.3 presents their cost estimates. For perspective, note that Canada's GDP in 1990 was approximately $700 billion.

The total figure that the Canadian researchers arrived at is quite large – the equivalent of around 1.7 percent of the country's gross domestic product (GDP). Nevertheless, it is important to realize that this estimate significantly understates the full costs of adaptation, as the study looked only at public expenditures and only at the federal level. More importantly, they did not include what households and firms spend to adapt to the cold. That is, they ignore the costs that households and firms bear privately[11] and, given that Canada is a market economy, we would expect that these would be quite significant.[12]

Even if we were able to calculate the full costs of adaptation this would still leave us short of measuring the full costs of the cold, however, because adaptation is never complete. Not all climate effects can be avoided by expenditures on adaptation, moreover. It will still be cold and this will still impose direct costs. To obtain an estimate of the full cost we would need to include, in addition to the full adaptation expenditures, at least three main categories of direct costs: (1) the impact on productive activities ranging from agriculture, forestry, and fishing, to manufacturing, and so on; (2) the impact on human health and mortality; and (3) the impact on human well-being and comfort apart from health – the so-called amenities effect. Canada may spend a lot on adapting to its climate, but Canadians still also choose to locate in ways that reduce their exposure to the cold, primarily by locating close to the US border, where the temperature is warmer.[13]

Suppose, however, that we could calculate the full cost of the cold to Canada. We would still be one step short, as what is necessary for our

Table 3.3 What Canada spends in a year to adapt to its cold

Sector	Cost of climate adaptation in billions of 1990 Canadian dollars per year
Transport	1.7
Construction	2.0
Agriculture	1.3
Forestry	0.4
Water	0.8
Household expenditure	5.3
Other	0.2
Total, all sectors	11.7

Source: Herbert and Burton (1994).

exercise is not the total cost but the cost per unit of temperature in order to calculate the cold costs to Russia of its location policies.

Today it is much easier to find studies about the costs of global warming than about the costs of increasing cold. Four decades ago, however, most experts were concerned about global cooling. Consequently, in the early 1970s the US Department of Transportation sponsored a series of conferences to study the effects of climate change on the economy and on human well-being. The resulting study, in which researchers were commissioned to study the effects of a cooling of 2 °C, is the only one that explicitly looks at the costs of cold for the US economy. In addition to the costs of damage to (reduced value of) the economy's production sectors, such as agriculture, forestry, and marine resources, and the extra costs of residential and industrial heating, specialists provided estimates of the costs to human health and comfort. The health costs included expenses for physicians' services, hospital visits, and drugs. Separately, they estimated the number of excess deaths that could be attributed to the cold. Finally, they looked at the cost to human beings of living and working in cold temperatures as expressed in differences in wages among urban areas in the US.[14]

Table 3.4 summarizes the findings from the DOT study.[15] We have converted them into costs per 1 °C, in billions of 1990 dollars. The total amount – roughly $60–85 billion – is equivalent to approximately 1.0 to 1.5 percent of 1990 US GDP.[16] This is essentially the additional costs to the economy if national TPC were reduced by 1 °C. This is a quite large cost, especially since it is incurred each year. For instance, an American economy that would normally expect to grow at an average of 3 percent per year over a 30-year period would sacrifice about 25–35 percent of that cumulative growth for a 1 °C decline in TPC.[17]

Table 3.4 What cold costs the US economy each year

Activity	*Costs per °C in billions of 1990 dollars*
Heating	4.9
Health impacts	14.8
Agriculture, forestry, fishing	14.4
Wages	16.2 (10.3 – 34.4)
Human life	16.0
Total	66.3 (60.4 – 84.5)
Cost as % of 1990 GDP	1.14 (1.04 – 1.46)

Source: Authors' calculations based on Anderson (1974), D'Arge (1974), and Hoch (1977).

How applicable to Russia?

These findings apply to the United States economy. Are they relevant for Russia? There are many problems involved in comparing anything to do with the US and Russian economies, but we can mention two major issues of relevance here. The first is the relationship between the gross cost of the cold in the two economies and the efficiency of measures taken to adapt to the cold. The second issue is the very different range of temperatures at which the costs of the cold would have to be assessed in Russia and the United States.

With respect to the first: if one spends a dollar in the US to adapt to the cold, what is the payoff, in terms of reduced damage or direct costs? What is the return to one dollar similarly invested in Russia? An area where this is particularly relevant is the assessment of the health and mortality costs of the cold. Americans spend huge sums to protect their health and treat their illnesses of all kinds, including those possibly caused by the cold. Russians clearly do not spend as much, even as a share of their much lower national income. But that lower spending (and consequent lower level of health care) presumably leads to higher mortality rates. The US is estimated to suffer 16,000 excess deaths per degree of cold. Pro-rated for population, that would imply about 9,000 annual excess Russian deaths per degree of cold. But do Russians die from cold at the same rates as Americans?

Then there is the issue of the economic value of each life lost. Economists' cost-of-life calculations are based on estimates of what an individual could have been expected to earn over the remainder of his or her working life. (Those lifetime earnings are taken as the value of a person's contribution to the economy.) This means that we would have to adjust for Russians' expected longevity as well as their specific earnings structure. These considerations imply that we cannot simply transfer the US findings to Russia without making significant adjustments to account for different conditions. It would be wise to use the American results only as a very general indicator that cold in any temperate or cold country undoubtedly has costs. But to determine precisely what those costs are would require an elaborate study of Russian conditions.

The need for further research is even more compelling when our second reservation is considered: namely that the countries' temperature ranges differ so much. The US estimates are for the cost of a degree of cold at the current US TPC, which, of course, is considerably warmer than Russia's. The issue here is that the cold-cost function is clearly non-linear.[18] The magnitude of the effect will not be the same at −12 °C as at +3 °C or +4 °C. But how much different would it be? Cold engineering suggests that at least some of the costs associated with the cold are in fact larger per degree at lower temperatures. It is clear, for example, from Figure 3.3 that a drop in temperature from −20 °C to −25 °C has a much greater effect on human and machine efficiency than a change in temperature from −5 °C to −10 °C. And the drop in productivity seems quite severe when the temperature drops from −25 °C to −30 °C.

An even more serious consideration is what happens when the thermometer drops below certain critical cold thresholds that trigger massive and disastrous materials failures. Even if the distribution of temperatures is independent of mean temperature, with a lower TPC Russia would be expected to experience more very cold days than the US, and some of the costs of adaptation are related to what happens at the extremes of temperature. For most of the populated world the extreme cold thresholds are, fortunately, not relevant, but Russia is different, and nowhere are these critical thresholds more of a daily reality for more people than in Siberia. It is not surprising that the most systematic study of the cold thresholds has been made by Russians, for the purpose of determining whether Siberian regions needed machines of special design or whether standard machines could somehow be modified through the addition of special parts made of cold-resistant steels. A compilation of the behavior of machines at various Siberian temperature levels gives a harrowing picture.[19] Some of the details are presented in Table 3.5.

Table 3.5 suggests that there is a "seismic" component to very cold temperatures: extreme discrete events have the effect of an earthquake.

Table 3.5 Cold thresholds in Siberia

Temp (°C)	Effect on standard Soviet machinery
−6	Internal combustion engines require pre-start engine heaters
−10	Destruction of some standard metal dredge components
−15	High-carbon steels break; car batteries must be heated; first critical threshold for standard equipment
−20	Standard compressors with internal combustion engines cease to operate; standard excavator hilt beams break; destruction of some tower crane components, dredging buckets, and bulldozer blades
−25 to −30	Unalloyed steels break; car-engine space, fuel, and oil tanks must be insulated; frost-resistant rubber required; non-frost resistant belts and standard pneumatic hoses break; some cranes fail
−30	Minimum temperature for use of any standard equipment
−30 to −35	Trestle cranes fail; some tractor shoes break
−35 to −40	Tin-alloyed steel components (ballbearings, etc.) shatter; saw frames and circular saws stop work; all compressors stop work; standard steels and structures rupture on mass scale

Source: Adapted from Mote (1983, p. 22) whence from Dogayev (1969, pp. 29–31).

This suggests that it is not just the mean temperature that is important. For cost analysis, therefore, one would want to know the extent and frequency of extreme cold. That is, how cold can it get, and how often does that happen? To analyze the extreme temperature component of the overall temperature profile of a location, we created the notion of a cold decile. This is the temperature that marks the coldest 10 percent of all days in the period recorded. Our research suggests that in most of Russia the cold decile cut-off value is roughly 10 °C lower than the mean. In other words, at any given mean January temperature it can be expected that, 10 percent of the time, the mean daily temperature will actually be 10 °C below the monthly mean. For instance, the city of Omsk in Siberia has a January mean of –19 °C. But on average, for three days each January the temperature will be below –29 °C. This means that the economic costs of very cold temperatures may be significantly understated if we look only at the mean January temperature of Omsk. The costs of adaptation and adjustment to cold may really be due to the frequency of these extremely cold days. The cold needs to cause the railroad trestle to break only one time to have a disastrous effect.

Counterfactual exercise

We have examined estimates of the cost of cold per degree using US data. Given that Russian TPC is significantly below that in the US, and that the costs are likely to be non-linear, the costs per degree are likely to be higher in Russia. But when we compare US and Russian TPC, we know that it is composed of two parts: the unavoidable climate and the avoidable location decisions. We would like to know how much of Russia's extreme cold was avoidable – and therefore at least in theory could be reversed. To do this, a counterfactual exercise is needed. We have to ask what Russian location decisions would have looked like if the choices of the Soviet period had been avoided.

We will draw on findings by Mikhailova (2004), who performed such a counterfactual experiment. Mikhailova's innovative approach to this problem was to take the location structure of Russia on the eve of World War I as a baseline and then use a model of location to predict where Russians would have ended up if the economy had evolved according to market economy principles in the twentieth century. Since Canada has a climate and resource base similar to that of Russia, she argued, a model of location with respect to cold estimated on Canadian data can produce the parameter estimates needed for the counterfactual exercise. Her approach therefore used Canadian data to estimate a model that characterizes the dynamic links between, on one hand, the spatial structure of the economy and, on the other hand, initial conditions and regional characteristics. With this estimated behavior model of the spatial dynamics in a market economy in hand, she then applied it to Russian initial conditions and endowments.[20] Her results show that the post-Soviet allocation of population and industry in Russia is very different from what would have occurred in the absence of Soviet location policy. It is colder and further to the east: that is, the eastern part of the country is noticeably overpopulated compared to the counterfactual market allocation, while the western part experiences a relative population deficit. The excess population in the Siberian and Far Eastern regions ranges from 9.6 to 17.6 million people according to various estimates (compared with an actual population of 34 million).[21] Figure 3.4 compares the actual path of TPC in Russia with the forecast of Mikhailova's counterfactual market model. The differences are significant. Without Soviet location policies TPC rises in Russia, as it did in Canada during the twentieth century.

Mikhailova then proceeds to estimate the cost to the Russian economy of the excess population in cold-climate regions. To calculate the cold-related cost of spatial inefficiency, she first investigates the relationship between temperature and various regional characteristics (energy consumption, health indicators, and productivity). She estimates the temperature elasticities of these characteristics and uses these estimates together with the measure of extra cold resulting from Soviet investment decisions – a difference of 1.5 °C in TPC – to calculate the cost in terms of present-day Russian GDP.

The costs Mikhailova finds are dramatic, even in the most cautious of her estimates (2004: 63–4):

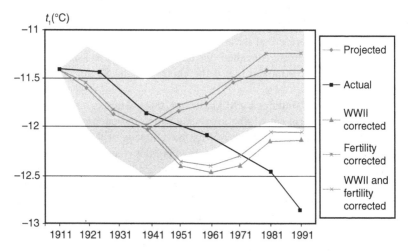

Figure 3.4 Mikhailova's projected and actual TPC dynamics in Russia

[This] difference in TPC costs not less than 1% of GDP in extra energy costs, and 0.2% of GDP in lost productivity in the construction sector alone annually. If all manufacturing industries had the same temperature elasticity of TFP as construction, loss of another 1.3% of GDP yearly could be attributed to cold. An additional 0.85% of aggregate mortality is also a direct consequence of Soviet spatial policy. These are annual costs, but compounded over the last 30 years of the Soviet era – a time when the spatial evolution of Russian economy took a sharpest detour from the optimal trajectory – they lead to a GDP loss in excess of 35% (or 97% in the worst-case scenario). Every person in Russia gave up at least one-fourth (or maybe a half) of his income for Siberian development!

These are dramatic costs, but it is important to note that Mikhailova only establishes a lower bound, since she was able to estimate only a portion of the costs. For example, she assumed that residential electricity consumption was independent of temperature, but it is almost certainly the case that in Russia electricity use rises as temperature falls.

Distance

Spatial misallocation in Russia is a product of vast size and past location mistakes. Russia's enormous territory, combined with the poor quality and quantity of its road networks, exacerbates the consequences of spatial misallocation. Distance increases the cost of transportation and, combined with inefficient location, raises the costs of production and consumption compared with an identical economy with efficient spatial location. Russia's vast size allows for vast mistakes.

Size, or distance, is like cold. It is an obstacle to overcome, and it is costly to do so. Some aspects of this are God-given. But, like the concept of "economic temperature," economic distance can be increased or decreased by location policies. It is not necessary to locate economic activity uniformly through the territory of a country. In the Soviet Union, however, location policies were not always guided by economic reality, and geopolitical motivations often predominated. Hence it would be interesting to conduct an exercise analogous to that undertaken above in relation to cold to estimate the extra cost from distance that was produced by Soviet policies. In this regard, it might seem that we could perform a similar counterfactual exercise to that which Mikhailova carried out for cold. All that would be needed would be to calculate an analog to TPC – call it DPC (distance per-capita) – and then use Mikhailova's counterfactual population distribution to calculate the extra DPC that Russia experiences owing to past decisions. Then, if we could calculate the cost of transporting goods, we could estimate a cost of excess distance for Russia.

It turns out, however, that the problem of distance is not so simple, because, unlike TPC, the analog measure for distance does not make much sense. It might seem that a compact country, one in which distances among economic actors are small, has an advantage. It is cheaper to transport goods and services and to conduct transactions.[22] This would be all there is to say if economies were closed. But suppose a country trades with other countries. Then proximity to those markets and suppliers might be more important than being close to those at home. Minimizing internal distances is not the solution to any practical economic problem for economies that trade.[23]

The complexity associated with distance can be illustrated by the following exercise. Suppose we measure the average distance between any two agents in a country. If everyone lived in the same city, for instance, the average distance would be close to zero. If the entire population is divided into two equal-sized cities 1,000 km apart, the average distance would be 500 km, and so on. In other words, distance per-capita (DPC) is the average distance between each resident of a country and all other residents. In practice, a calculation that included the entire population (or even just all cities) would be a gigantic exercise. We calculated the DPC for several large industrialized countries using the 50 largest cities in each.[24] To account for the differences in the countries' total territory, we divide each country's DPC by its area. The results are displayed in Figure 3.5.

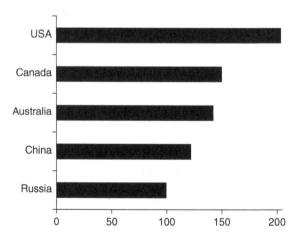

Figure 3.5 Average distance per-capita relative to country size

Note: The measure is a dimensionless index, DPC ("distance per-capita"), divided by land area.

At first glance the results in Figure 3.5 may seem surprising. Russia, despite being much larger than the United States or Canada, has a far smaller relative DPC. Two randomly selected Americans are on average twice as far apart as two Russians relative to the countries' size.[25] Upon reflection, the reason for this apparently puzzling result is obvious: in the United States, population is dispersed according the value of the location economically. Population is dense along the coasts because that facilitates trade with the rest of the world. Russia, which is much less open economically, has less of its population located along its borders and more of it distributed in the interior. Russia has occupied much of the interior with larger cities to satisfy inward orientations and to occupy territory.[26] Thus, it could be argued that what relative DPC is measuring is not spatial efficiency but an *aversion to empty space.*

That aversion to empty space especially manifests itself in the way Russia has populated its least inhabitable places. Suppose we compare population densities in Eastern Siberia and the Russian Far East with those of Alaska and northern Canada in terms of their relative shares of total national population and territory. If Alaska had been populated according to the Russian model, it would have today not 710,000 residents, but 13 million. Canada's Northwest Territory and Yukon Territory would together have 1.5 million residents instead of the 79,000 they actually have. Conversely, if Eastern Siberia and the Russian Far East had followed the American and Canadian patterns, they would in total have barely 1 million residents instead of their current 15 million.

In a normal market economy, the trend is toward agglomeration – concentration of economic activity – rather than even distribution across space. As Hall (1991: 5) points out,

> [if] there are costs of moving products from one place to another, [then] producers and consumers will locate themselves close to each other. Along a line drawn almost anywhere on land, economic activity (GNP per square foot) will vary by many orders of magnitude. Agglomeration tends to occur at natural ports and other salient geographic points.

Hence, across countries the distribution of population will depend on country-specific factors that determine their patterns of agglomeration.

Distance or size *per se*, therefore, is not the issue. A country that is territorially large will have big distance costs. If it has resources (and that is true for many large countries), they will be bulk commodities transported over great spaces. There will, therefore, be some necessary transport costs. But the extra cost comes not from geography alone but from the location of people and cities in an economic sense. The question is whether the population is distributed efficiently, given the potential for agglomeration in the country. Canada provides an instructive contrast to Russia. Its resource-rich northern provinces are only one-twelfth as densely populated as Russia's eastern regions. The question we must then ask is: How well-suited is Russia's transportation structure to its population, which is highly dispersed across a vast space?

Russia's transport infrastructure

In light of Russia's spatial misallocation, the efficiency of the transportation system is crucial. Can it make up for the handicap Russia faces as a result of the factors of cold and distance? Some evidence on transport infrastructure relative to country size is given in Table 3.6, which presents totals for area, population, roads, rail lines, and vehicles, along with relative measures for Russia and other large countries.

Table 3.6 Comparative country sizes and transport infrastructure

	Quantities				
	Land area (km² millions)	Population (millions)	Roads (km millions)	Vehicles (millions)	Rail lines (km 000)
Russia	16.4	142	0.937	37	84.2
China	9.3	1325	3.770	49	60.8
USA	9.1	304	4.169	158	227.1
Canada	9.1	33	1.440	20	57.2
Brazil	8.5	192	n.a.	40	29.8
Australia	7.7	21	0.821	15	9.7

	Densities				
	Population/ area (persons per km²)	Roads/area (km per km² 000)	Vehicles/ population (per 1,000)	Vehicles/ roads (per km)	Rail lines/ area (km per km² 000)
Russia	8.7	57	264	40	5.1
China	142.0	404	37	13	6.5
USA	33.2	456	521	38	24.8
Canada	3.7	158	605	14	6.3
Brazil	22.6	n.a.	209	n.a.	3.5
Australia	2.8	107	687	18	1.3

Source: Authors' calculations from World Bank data.

The data in Table 3.6 demonstrate Russia's transport handicap relative to other large countries. Russia relies heavily on rail transport (see Table 3.7), yet its figure for rail lines per square kilometer is much smaller than the US, and also smaller than that for Canada or China.

Table 3.7 appears to show that Russia and the US rely on rail transport to roughly similar degrees. But this is somewhat misleading, because so much oil in Russia is shipped by pipeline. Thus, if pipeline shipments are taken out then the dominance of rail in Russia is more evident. Rail accounts for 85 percent of non-pipeline freight in Russia, but 47 percent in the US. Thirty-nine percent of non-pipeline freight in the US is shipped by truck, versus only 9 percent in Russia. This is perhaps the most striking comparison. The reason is the deficiency in Russia's roads, both in terms of quantity and quality.

It is evident from Table 3.6 that Russia's total road network is smaller than that of China or the US. When the road network is measured relative to the size of the territory the differences are quite dramatic. One might argue that the density of Russia's road network in terms of its territory is not informative: if there is a lot of empty space then this measure will be misleading. But Russia's size is not what accounts for the disparity. To see this, we redo the comparison by ignoring Siberia. That is, suppose we truncate Russia at the Urals, keeping only the westernmost 30 percent of the country. That would leave a territory that is only around 55 percent as large as the continental United States. Even this much smaller Russia has an average road density (km of roads per 1,000 square km of territory) of around 150, compared to over 800 in the continental United States and over 400 in China.

Clearly, Russia needs more roads. But it also needs higher-capacity roads and better quality roads. From 1960 to 1990 Russia expanded its road network more than five-fold (see Figure 3.6). But that was from a very low base and even at the end of the period total road mileage in Russia was still only 18 percent of that in the United States. Adjusted for

Table 3.7 US and Russian freight transport system by mode of shipment (percent of total kilometer-tons shipped)

	US	Russia
Rail	37.0	43.0
Truck	31.0	4.4
Water	11.0	3.0
Air	<1.0	<1.0
Pipeline	21.0	50.0

Note: US data 2008, Russian data 2009.

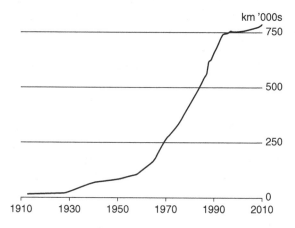

Figure 3.6 Growth of Russia's road network, 1913–2010

Source: GKS.

Russia's larger size, Russia's coverage was only 10 percent of that of the US. Moreover, these statistics do not account for the quality of the roads or even their width (number of lanes). Most of Russia's roads are one- or two-lane roads; of the total of nearly 800,000 km of roads, only 4,300 km are roads with four or more lanes. That is around 1.2 percent of the US total of such highways.[27]

The upshot of this discussion is that Russia has greater transportation needs than other large countries, yet it possesses a less efficient transportation infrastructure. This imposes a cost on economic activity. As we noted in Chapter 2, inefficiency in the production of intermediate goods has a multiplier effect on productivity. Costly transportation is exactly the type of factor that introduces wedges that are multiplied through stages of production. This means that for goods that are produced with identical technologies and identical stocks of capital and labor, Russia will produce less output than its competitors. This will show up as lower productivity. It will appear that Russia produces less because of the organization of production, but in fact the lower productivity is due to the legacy of past spatial decisions. This handicap will not be eliminated by changes in organization form.

Should Russia then focus its resources on modernizing its transport network? In the typical country with such an inadequate network, the returns to such investment would be high. But it is important to think about the problem more carefully in the case of Russia. While improvements in transportation infrastructure will have cost-reducing effects, they will do nothing to eliminate the burden of a highly dispersed population and the lack of empty space. Building a transportation network to minimize the costs of the current spatial location is a bear trap. Even a cost-minimizing, efficient transportation system cannot eliminate the burden of running an economy that is spatially misallocated. In fact, it would likely deepen the problem in the long term. Such a system would still be needlessly high-cost relative to its competitors abroad.[28] A policy of this sort ignores the opportunity cost of the cities. If the cities should not be there, building more roads to them makes things worse. It is not a sunk cost. If it were, it could just be written off as a mistake. But expanding the transport infrastructure to connect cities over vast distances reinforces the original mistake and creates even more costs in future. Even more wasteful than the "Bridge to Nowhere" is a "Bridge to Somewhere that Should Not Exist." Rather than spending money to build more and better roads to connect non-economic locations, policy should be directed at phasing out those locations, making them less important. Resources could instead be used to better link cities and people that are more rationally located.

Post-Soviet correction?

One might argue that Russia has had 20 years to undo some of the location decisions of the Soviet period. Perhaps the rise of a market economy has led this situation to correct itself? After the collapse of the command-administrative system of economic management in the early 1990s, free market forces in Russia began correcting the spatial misallocation that had occurred during the Soviet era. People migrated out of the coldest and most remote regions. That self-adjustment came to a halt in 1999. This is evident in Figure 3.7 which displays the change in TPC by year. If people left colder climates and moved to more economically active locations with warmer temperatures we would observe TPC rising. Hence, as Richard Ericson has pointed out (pers. comm.) the change in TPC can be interpreted as an index of economic rationality. If TPC rises, location is becoming more rational. This process is evident in the first years of economic reform but has been reversed over the last decade as a result of policy. Plans for Siberian development and repopulation are back on the national agenda. For example, in June 2006 Vladimir Putin announced a new migration program designed to attract ethnic Russians from abroad to return to Russia in order to repopulate Siberia and the East.[29]

Overall geographical mobility remains quite low in Russia, something that impedes reallocation of human capital. The total number of internal migrants in Russia – that is, people who changed their city or district

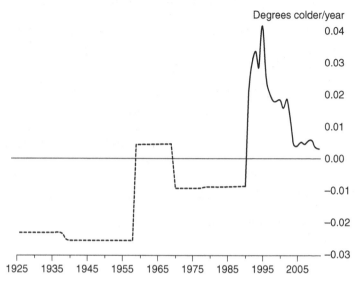

Figure 3.7 Russia's economic cooling/warming rate, 1926–2011(annual rate of change in TPC)

Source: Authors' calculations from GKS regional populations, temperatures.

[*rayon*] of residence during the year – fell from 3.3 million in 1992 to 1.7 million in 2009.[30] Russia's internal migration rate is now only about 1.2 percent.[31] The comparable rates for the United States and Canada are over 5 percent. In an economy that needs much more dynamism, this trend towards less mobility is not good. Yet Russian leaders are trying to block the little mobility that there is as they argue against the depopulation of Siberia.[32] The call for policies to reverse population movements from Siberia is one of the most significant bear traps in Russia today.

Conclusion

The costs to Russia of its location, and of its location policies – both the immutable and the self-induced problems – are severe. They are a tax on Russian growth, and they are a potential bear trap if they are not understood correctly. It is tempting to think that, given the industrial resources in many of the very cold cities, Russia should invest its wealth to modernize these structures. With enough investment, it is possible to adapt to the cold. With sufficient investment, you can make anything viable. As we noted in *Russia's Virtual Economy* (2002: 7):

Of course, a sufficient infusion of outside resources can guarantee successful restructuring for any enterprise, because this makes it possible to reconstruct the entire enterprise from scratch. Therefore, any meaningful notion of restructuring has to consider the opportunity cost of making a given enterprise viable.

But if one is to invest sufficient resources to rebuild an enterprise, why do that in Perm rather than Rostov? Even with zero cost of capital it would not make economic sense to re-invest in Perm.[33] Cities with better climate and location, such as Rostov or some similarly warmer (for Russia) city, would make much better choices. To rebuild in Perm it is necessary to have directed capital subsidies. When Russia spends money on replacing worn-out infrastructure in Siberian and Urals cities that are far colder than urban centers of that size anywhere else in the world, when it builds roads to connect cities whose very existence no market economy would have tolerated, when it channels investment into factories that were not located, equipped, and staffed with even the foggiest idea of a market in mind – when it makes these and hundreds and thousands of other similar investment decisions, it is not only wasting the very scarce resources it has available today but also dooming future generations to continue the waste.

Why does this location problem persist? The Soviet Union was dismantled in 1991 and a market economy has replaced central planning, yet the legacy of the Soviet period in terms of location policy persists. To explain this, we must turn to political economy, especially the implications of federalism Russia style, which we do in the next chapter.

Appendix: economics of space distortion

We have emphasized the handicap imposed by distance. In this appendix we discuss the economics of space distortion. In particular, we examine the implications for measurement of ignoring this distortion.

Consider an economy with given quantities of capital, labor, and technology. All activity takes place at a point. There is a given level of output, Y, that is feasible. All of this is available for consumption and investment, so it produces a given welfare level. Call this level of output Y^*.

Now suppose the economy is stretched out. It expands spatially. It is now necessary to ship goods across space to make production feasible. Hence, some of the factors of production must be used to transport inputs and outputs. Hence, with the given levels of primary factors, and with the given level of technology, final output must fall. Welfare is lower in this economy because the environment contains these new spatial constraints. But if producers are profit maximizers they will locate activity to minimize transportation costs. Thus, output is now the maximum feasible given these constraints and is efficient subject to the constraints of spatial dispersion. Call this new level of output $\hat{Y}$. Clearly we have $\hat{Y} < Y^*$.

Now compare this with an alternative economy with the same level of capital, labor, and technology, but a different spatial dispersion. Specifically, in this alternative economy producers are not cost minimizers. In this spatial misallocation production is no longer on the production frontier. More of the capital and labor must be used for transportation, so output is now even lower, $\overline{Y} < \hat{Y}$. The difference between these two levels $\hat{Y} - \overline{Y} \equiv \gamma$ represents the loss due to spatial misallocation. Clearly, the potential for this loss is greater the larger the country and the more location decisions were due to non-economic motives (politics, fear of the enemy, etc.).

Let us now consider a comparison of total factor productivity (TFP) between these two economies. The only difference between them is spatial allocation. We know that $\hat{Y}$ is greater than $\overline{Y}$, but since capital, labor, and production are the same in both economies we will find that measured TFP in the alternative (spatially misallocated) economy is lower than in the one with an efficient spatial allocation, i.e. $\overline{A} \leq \hat{A}$. Normally, one would attribute such a finding to lower innovation or less productivity or technological sophistication in the alternative economy. To close the gap policymakers would typically recommend some variant of "modernization" or "innovation." But in fact the difference is entirely due to misallocation of production across space, by construction. Modernization of production will not close the gap since their "technology" levels are the same by assumption, even though TFP differs.

The reason that we typically ignore the spatial loss factor, γ, is that for most economies location decisions are assumed to be efficient. We assume that the economy is on its production frontier, so output changes over time depend on more inputs or an improvement in technology. But if a country has spatial misallocation then it is inside the frontier, and what looks like low productivity may be just a wedge due to location legacies.

4 Market-impeding federalism

> Muscovites should live well. Everyone else should think about Russia, so the Muscovites can live even better.[1]

Introduction

We have seen that Russia suffers greatly from the legacy of spatial misallocation: too many people, and too much capital, in the wrong places. This would not be so bad if internal labor migration were high. In fact, however, it has been and remains very low.[2] To understand why this legacy persists, we now turn our attention to the federal structure of Russia. Post-Soviet Russia imposed a formal federal structure on a spatial distribution of productive forces that was non-market. The federalism became market-impeding rather than, as had been intended, market-promoting. We refer to the peculiar Russian policy that federalism helped produce as "lights on" Our argument in this chapter is that the policy of "lights on" plays a central role in the conservation of the legacies from the Soviet period, reducing mobility of both labor and capital. Given its importance in the political economy of Russia, it is worth developing the argument in full.

Federalism is to be distinguished from decentralization. Governance of any territorially large country requires some decentralization. Non-democratic societies typically use an administrative-hierarchical system of decentralization. Democracies, in contrast, rely on some notion of federalism – that is, a regional distribution of political power. Typically, the power distribution is related to the regions' economic importance as reflected in their population sizes.

Some have argued that federalism offers potential advantages for countries trying to reform. First, it allows for experimentation and competition among jurisdictions with regard to policies. Successful policies by innovating regions will be emulated by others. Second, a federal structure may serve as a check on central government interference in the economy. Federalism, it has been said, is a "governance solution of the state to credibly preserve market incentives."[3] The example of China is often used to illustrate how market-preserving federalism works. In contrast, Russia, which is also a federal state, is often criticized for failing to implement market-preserving incentives. In this chapter we will show what can happen when federalism is implemented in an economy such as Russia, in which the initial allocation of resources across regions is non-economic. Under those circumstances, federalism will not serve to preserve markets unless it promotes reallocation of factors. In fact, however, this is not the case in Russia, where mobility of both capital and labor is low. It may not be surprising that capital is relatively immobile in Russia, but, contrary to what one might think, in Russia labor is even less mobile.[4] Apparently, investment/disinvestment decisions produce more variation in the regional capital stock than interregional migration does for regional labor forces.[5] A cross-sectional series of regional capital stocks in 1994 and in 2000 display a correlation of 92.6 percent,[6] while the series of regional labor forces are correlated at the 99.8 percent level.[7] In this chapter we try to explain this rigidity in the locational distribution of both capital and labor, linking it to the phenomenon of federalism.

Predation and capture

The most compelling argument in favor of federalism as a promoter of economic development is that it limits predation by central government on economic actors. As Weingast (1995: 1) notes, any government that is strong enough to protect property rights is also strong enough to confiscate wealth. Consequently, whatever commitment such a government makes not to predate may be called into question. Decentralization of authority, however, limits the information available to central authorities. Because this in turn raises the cost of predation and therefore enhances the credibility of commitments not to predate, federalist decentralization leads to improved market incentives.

If it is true that federalism serves to restrain the predatory instincts of central governments, this raises the question: Why do some governments with federal structures predate more than others? Why, for example, has the private sector developed more in China than Russia? Both countries have federal institutions. Blanchard and Shleifer (2001) developed a simple model to answer this question. They put forward two hypotheses to explain the greater level of predation in Russia:

- Local government is captured by older firms. As a result, local governments work to generate transfers to older firms and to protect them from new competitors.

- Local officials compete for rents from the new business sector. The proliferation of agencies trying to extract rents from new private firms stifles the growth of the local economy.

But why are these forces weaker in China? Blanchard and Shleifer offer two explanations. First, they argue that initial rent claimants were weaker in China than in Russia. This is partly due to the level of development in the two countries and the nature of economic structures. Second, the central government in China was stronger. The Communist Party remained intact. Blanchard and Shleifer focus on the consequences of the latter explanation. However, they do not consider the nature of the federal system itself. We augment their analysis by asking the question: What happens if the political boundaries in a federal system are inappropriate economic units?

The Blanchard–Shleifer model

Since we use the Blanchard–Shleifer model as a basis for much of the analysis in this chapter, it is useful to set out the model in some detail. It posits a government that has two levels: central and local. Each local government has a simple choice:

- It can foster growth by limiting transfers of resources to state and former state firms and allowing new private firms to enter and grow.
- It can kill growth by transferring resources to old firms and/or preventing new firms from being created.

Why would a local government choose to kill growth? Under the capture view it is straightforward: old firms dictate local government policy to their advantage. Under the competition for rent view, the local government is simply unable to prevent the escalation of bribes and corruption that stifle all new business. Both views have the same negative implications for growth.[8]

We begin by fixing notation. Let y be the additional output if there is growth, and normalize this so that it also stands for the additional amount of revenue available to the central and local governments with growth. Let b be the private benefits to the local government of killing growth. Under the capture view this could be transfers back from existing firms.[9] Under the rents interpretation it could be the cost to local officials of trying to stop bribe-taking.

Now let us turn to the central government. It is assumed to prefer growth, and it has a carrot and a stick to help it achieve its objectives. *Revenue sharing* is the carrot. The central government can choose the extent to which it shares revenue with the local government. Let α be the share of revenues from additional growth going to the local government.[10] If the local government chooses to foster growth, it gets αy.[11] Normalize this so that it also measures how much the local government values growth. Note that it is *ex post* α that is crucial. *Political centralization* is the stick. The central government influences whether the local government can stay in power. Let p_x be the probability that the local government stays in power if it kills growth, and p_y be the probability that it stays in power if it fosters growth. The value of p_x will clearly depend on how local officials are chosen. In China the central government can choose p_x freely. In Russia, there were elections for these positions for the first decade and a half of transition, so p_x depends on how effective the central government is at influencing elections. Since 2005 Putin has appointed the governors, so in principle, p_x can be chosen as freely in Russia as in China.[12]

Now we define $p = p_y/p_x$. In other words, p is an index that measures the efficacy of the central government's stick with regard to governors. The higher the value of p, the greater the penalty for not engaging in pro-reform policies. Notice that the stick is limited, in the sense that the maximum penalty for the governor is loss of his job.[13] For the prospects of market reform, it would be desirable to have p greater than one. But if the center has little control over outcomes, and if capture is important, then it may be less than one.

A further important assumption in Blanchard and Shleifer is that regions do not differ. Hence, it makes sense to assume uniform values of α, p, and y.[14] Under these assumptions, the local government chooses growth if the expected payoff for pro-growth policies is greater than the benefit of killing growth, or

$$p_y \alpha y > p_x b$$

or

$$p \alpha y > b \tag{4.1}$$

Expression (4.1) says that the local government is more likely to choose growth the stronger the stick (high p), the larger the carrot (higher α), the larger the growth potential (y), and the smaller the benefits of not reforming (b).[15]

Proponents of the federalist position often focus on the fiscal problems of the center, which renegotiates its stake and cannot commit. They argue that market-preserving federalism provides better incentives. By this logic, the differences in economic performance between China and Russia are explained by differences in α.[16] Blanchard and Shleifer argue that the empirical evidence suggests that α may be lower in Russia than

China but that this is not altogether clear. One complication is that there are actually three levels of subnational governments in Russia, and most of the empirical work has focused on the bottom two.[17] There certainly appears to be a high level of fiscal transfers. There are few taxpaying regions and many recipients of subsidies. In China, the evidence seems to indicate a value of α close to 0.8. Although this may suggest that there is more redistribution in China, Blanchard and Shleifer argue that differences in α are probably too small to explain the differences in performance.

Blanchard and Shleifer note that p also differs significantly between China and Russia. In China the Party still rules, so p is very high. In Russia, even after Putin's shift to appointed governors, Russia still lacked a party apparatus as in China; hence, the center cannot always get its way. So p is much lower, perhaps less than unity. In this environment improvements in α may have little effect. In other words, the economic benefits of federalism depend on a stick – some degree of centralization.[18] This suggests that differences in p could offset large improvements in α in the case of Russia. With high enough p, a high α may not even be necessary. The model suggests that to the extent that federalism has been important in promoting growth in China, such federalism relied crucially on the power of the Party. Greater democracy could mean much lower p. With a lower p, variation in α takes center stage.

Loser regions

The analysis of economic reform in the Blanchard–Shleifer model is predicated on the idea that all regions are uniform and hence that they all could benefit from reform. But what if regions are not uniform, but differ in their economic prospects? It is certainly true that market reforms would improve *efficiency* in any region, and certainly across regions. But it is not at all clear that reforms will necessarily lead to *growth* in all regions.[19] Obviously if y is small – if there are poor growth prospects – then it really does not matter much about carrots or sticks. If y is negative – if reform requires the region to contract – then matters are more complicated, and we turn to this analysis now.

In the Blanchard–Shleifer model appropriate federalism always leads to pro-growth policies. If p is raised high enough, it can always compensate for a low value of y. Blanchard–Shleifer move beyond the previous literature by showing that variation in α is insufficient to ensure that federalism will be growth inducing. But their analysis is based on the assumption that y is always positive: that is, that there is always a pro-growth reform that results in higher income in the region. This may seem an obvious assumption, but given the legacies of the Soviet period it may be that the best policies for some regions would require them to shrink. Welfare would be enhanced if they contracted.

It is also important to note that α is bounded from above by unity. The Blanchard–Shleifer model points out that there are thus limits to the carrots that the center can provide to governors. Indeed, that may be the central point. Moreover, even if $\alpha \rightarrow 1$, the actual carrot is limited by the size of y. If y is low, carrots are limited.[20] Notice that p, on the other hand, can go to infinity.[21]

It should be immediately apparent that if $y < 0$ – that is, if growth is negative – then a policy of high α provides no carrot. Indeed, in the case of a loser region governors would prefer to have $\alpha < 0$.[22] That is, they would want to be compensated for the loss – say, for example, in terms of tax revenue – incurred by adopting the pro-reform policies. Having a set of differentiated values of α is a move away from market federalism and towards discretion. To stay within the context of this literature, we keep α fixed and then consider side payments that may be needed to induce governors in loser regions to adopt reforms.

What does it mean to say that a pro-growth policy may cause $y < 0$? Consider a region whose location-specific endowment is so poor – relative to other regions – that adoption of market reforms would lead to a shift of labor and capital out of the region. Because of the legacy of the Soviet period, as we have explained in Chapter 3, regions that are distant from markets, are in very cold regions, and were over-industrialized in Soviet times may have very poor growth prospects. Indeed, owing to the nature of Soviet location policy these regions are not just uneconomic but may also be overpopulated.[23] In the case of such over-industrialized and overpopulated regions market liberalization may thus require the value of capital to be written off. The correct market response is for the region to shrink, for people to move out, and for $y < 0$. These are true loser regions.[24] If subsidies are eliminated, regional GDP (at least as measured) goes down. So the net change in taxable resources goes down. How does this change the analysis? We treat this in steps.

Inter-regional transfers

If in some regions j, $y_j < 0$, it follows that pro-growth policies will not be adopted even if a "perfect" form of federalism is chosen. That is, even setting $\alpha = 1$ and letting $p \rightarrow \infty$, condition (4.1) will not be satisfied for the loser region.[25] Pro-reform outcomes in loser regions are possible only if the winner regions buy them off. But this in turn means that α cannot be set as equal to one for all regions, since winner regions will have to contribute to the central treasury to compensate the loser regions. Winners would have an $\alpha < 1$.[26]

Consider the decision in loser region j. If that region is to choose pro-growth, a side payment will be needed to offset the negative value of y_j. For this region, $p\alpha y_j < b$. Therefore, a special transfer or side payment, ϕ, is needed, such that:[27]

$$p\,[\alpha y_j + \phi] \geq b_j \tag{4.2}$$

or

$$\phi \geq \frac{b_j}{p} - \alpha y_j \tag{4.3}$$

If (4.3) holds with equality, then ϕ is the minimum side payment required to get the loser region j to choose pro-growth.[28] This minimum payment depends positively on b_j, the personal benefit of not reforming, and on y_j, since the more the region must shrink the more the governor loses from reform. A bigger stick – higher p – reduces the magnitude of the side payment.

Notice that in this case we must already alter the model from "perfect" federalism. Now there is a cross-region budget constraint to consider. While $\alpha_j = 1$ is still feasible for the loser region, as indicated above, in regions that are winners we must have $\alpha_i < 1$ in order to finance the additional side payments. Suppose that there are only two regions. Then in region i (the "winner region"), we must have $\phi_j \leq (1 - \alpha_i)\, y_i$.[29] That is, the side payment to j is constrained by the revenue earned in region i, which depends on the tax rate in i $(1 - \alpha_i)$ and its gains from reform, y_i. The side payments are also constrained by the requirement that i has to have the incentive to reform, which takes place if:

$$p\alpha_i y_i > b_i. \tag{4.4}$$

In the two-region case a necessary condition for reform to be viable is that overall reform is efficient: $y_i > |\,y_j\,|$. That is, the marginal gains in winner region i must be greater than the losses in the loser region, and we assume that this is indeed the case.[30] Of course, this is not a sufficient condition for reform to be chosen, but this is the interesting case if we want to analyze when federalism may impede reforms. In the more general case, with many regions, the same type of condition is needed: that is, the gains in the winner regions must be at least as large as the losses (in absolute terms) in the loser regions.

Inter-regional migration

Does the introduction of differentiated side payments – ones that satisfy conditions (4.3) and (4.4) – suffice to ensure reform in both regions? Not necessarily. There are additional considerations for both loser and winner regions that result from the movement of factors caused by reforms. We consider these in turn.

Migration: loser regions

If a side payment induces reform in a loser region, that region will shrink both demographically and economically. A governor who considers only net income will choose reform. It may be, however, that governors of loser regions are not indifferent to shrinkage. Their status and prestige may depend on the size and importance of a region. Hence, from the viewpoint of the governor, reform may incur an additional non-pecuniary cost (future political status perhaps being paramount). Therefore, governors of loser regions may require payments larger than ϕ_j to choose reform, although we ignore them in our analysis in this chapter.

Migration: winner regions

Recall that pro-growth policies in loser region j lead to out-migration to the winner region, i. If productivity is higher in i this shift of excess labor to i will raise national income, as well as income in region i. However, it is crucial to note that migration will also impose additional costs on region i. These costs take the form of congestion costs, since land and infrastructure are given at any point in time.[31] There are also losses to workers due to downward pressure on wages. Of course, employers gain, but they are outnumbered by workers. On balance, the net gain could be positive or negative in the winner regions.[32] If the net gains were positive, we would expect Moscow to embrace immigration from the rest of Russia. Instead, we see the opposite, which suggests that congestion costs outweigh the benefits of immigration. Our assumption in the following is that net congestion costs are positive. Hence, let η_i be the net congestion costs imposed on region i from in-migration when region i chooses to reform.[33]

Given the potential for in-migration to cause congestion, we now need to modify the condition for reform in region i. Congestion creates an additional cost of reform. Reform in region i makes it more attractive to workers in other regions where reform has not taken place. Pro-growth is supported by i only if:

$$p(a_i y_i - \eta_i) > b_i \tag{4.5}$$

Whether (4.5) will be satisfied or not is open to question. But even if it is satisfied, and the governor of i is willing to reform despite being forced to pay an additional transfer to region j to reform, the payoff to reform is now lower. Clearly the size of η_i will matter. If there are many loser regions for each winner region, congestion costs could be large. Taken to an extreme, if there is a single winner region and many loser regions, the real and perceived congestion costs could be enormous.[34] In that case it may take a really big stick to ensure that region i chooses reform. There may, however, be an alternative. What if the winner region could figure out a way to prevent the loser region from reforming?

"Lights on"

Suppose that Moscow can make a side payment to region j that keeps enterprises open in j – keeps the lights on – and prevents out-migration. Region i no longer has to bear congestion costs and can reform without having to suffer from region j's reform.

Let θ_{ji} be the subsidy payment that i needs to make to keep the lights on in region j and prevent out-migration.[35] We know that region j, because it is a loser region, reforms only if it receives the side payment ϕ_j.[36] This side payment is observable by the governor of region i, so to prevent reform he will have to pay a subsidy of $\theta_{ji} \geq \phi_j$.[37] Notice that the size of this subsidy depends on what is going on in region j. From (4.4) we see that $\theta_{ji} \geq p_j a_j y_j - b_j$. The right-hand side of the inequality is independent of what is happening in the winner region i.

When is it advantageous for region i to make the subsidy payment to keep the lights on in loser region j? Comparing the payoffs to the winner region, we can see that region i will prefer "lights on" if

$$p_i(a_i y_i - \theta_{ji}) > p_i(a_i y_i - \eta_{ij}) \tag{4.6}$$

or, simply:[38]

$$\eta_{ij} > \theta_{ji} \tag{4.7}$$

Expression (4.7) is completely straightforward and intuitive. It simply says that region i is better off with the "lights on" strategy if and only if the congestion cost imposed by reform in region j is larger than the subsidy payment required to forestall reform.

If there are many loser regions Moscow may have to choose where to keep the lights on. Presumably regions could be ranked by the net benefit to Moscow of paying the subsidy payment: $\eta_{ij} - \theta_{ji} \equiv \gamma_{ij}$. Moscow could then choose to pay off regions in order.

If (4.7) holds, then region i reforms while the loser region does not reform, choosing instead to keep the lights on by utilizing the subsidy paid by region *i*. Moscow reforms and pays Perm to keep the lights on and prevent out-migration. Over time, this leads to an even greater divergence in economic performance across these regions. This increases the incentive for migration were Moscow to "turn off" the lights.[39] As Perm falls farther and farther behind Moscow it will require greater infusions to keep its citizens. As with addiction, the need for the subsidies increases over time. Hence, embarking on this path may create a trap where the winner region has to continually increase the size of its payments to keep the lights on.[40]

What we have demonstrated is that under reasonable conditions it makes sense for loser regions to resist reforms if the "lights on" subsidies from winner regions are sufficient. The key condition is that congestion costs in the winner region be high enough. Basically, the winner region pays a tax to keep population in the loser regions. As long as economic performance in the winner regions is not dependent on an inflow of labor this condition is likely to hold. The fact that Moscow has utilized a residence permit system to limit in-migration since the early days of economic reform suggests that this condition is likely satisfied.[41]

In our analysis we have followed the Blanchard–Shleifer model's assumption that the central government was in favor of reform in all regions. It was to this end – to achieve reform nationwide – that the central government used its sticks and carrots with respect to the regional governors. Governors were the agents who chose or rejected reform locally, depending on the relative weight of costs and benefits to them. Our "lights on" thesis added a further angle. We found that, under certain circumstances, a winner region that would be strongly in favor of reform in its own jurisdiction might prefer that *other* regions – loser regions – *not* reform, and it would be willing to act informally to give an incentive to these loser regions to refrain from reform in order to itself avoid the congestion costs that would result if loser regions reformed and laid off excess workers.

Our paradigmatic winner region in this situation was Moscow. But, owing to the special status of Moscow in Russia, the "lights on" argument may have consequences for the initial assumption about the central government's pro-reform attitude. Not only is Moscow's economic, social, and political weight greater by far than any other region's, but it is also the physical location of Russia's central government, and consequently of all the individuals who work for the government. Therefore, it is reasonable to assume that the policy preferences of Moscow will strongly influence national policy. Specifically, there will be a "lights on" bias in the central government as well. The central government will likely not merely turn a blind eye to Moscow's informal policy of supporting factories in loser regions; it will actively support Moscow's efforts. This would not be the case if the central government were located elsewhere – say, in Rostov.

Then Moscow would have to bear the full cost it incurs from loser-region reform on its own.

It is important to emphasize that we have investigated only economic factors that create incentives for the "lights on" policy. There may be political factors that also induce such payments, and in Chapter 6 we will examine just such a motive.

The "lights-on" mechanism

So far we have assumed that the subsidy payments are in cash. In practice, however, they take a distinctively non-cash form. Because they are intended to keep the lights on it is essential that they keep producers operating. We examine the implications of this crucial factor here.

To illustrate this subsidy mechanism we follow an example from Blanchard and Kremer's (1997) model of disorganization. Imagine that the economy is a chain of n enterprises (indexed by $l = 1,\dots, n$). Production is sequential, with each enterprise (l) using the output of the preceding enterprise ($l - 1$) as an input into its production. We modify the Blanchard–Kremer model to assume that each enterprise is in a different region, so there are n total regions as well. Region 1 produces a primary resource that is used in production by region 2, which produces an intermediate good used by region 3, and so on. At the end of n steps a good is produced that has value normalized to equal 1. Let the alternative value – the export value – of the primary resource be c.

In Blanchard–Kremer the value of producing in the chain is greater than the alternative value of the primary resource. One of the problems they analyze is inefficient bargaining over the surplus earned throughout the chain of production.[42] In their setup only $(1/2)^n - c$ is left at the first stage to split owing to bargaining at all stages further down the production chain. Let us suppose, however, that the value of production in the chain is less than the alternative value of the product. That is, $c > 1$. Then, with a market reform, it would be best to shut down production in the $n - 1$ regions and finance consumption out of exports alone.[43] Export of the primary product is more efficient. Reform thus raises y in the resource-producing region and reduces it in all the other regions. This is the quintessential example of winner and loser regions. Reform means less is wasted in the chain, so national GDP rises. But if the first region reforms and exports the primary product, all the other regions are devastated. It is quite easy to think of the first region as Tyumen Oblast, producing oil, and all other oblasts as industrial regions that process oil into products, for example.

If the country is a federalist structure then the center can force the winner region to compensate the losers. The efficient policy would be to tax the export and rebate some amount to each citizen in the loser region. But this will lead to all the congestion in the winner regions that we have just argued that the center wants to avoid, as there is no reason to stay in the loser regions if the enterprises are shut down there. Households can take their checks and move away. This is socially efficient – why pay the costs involved in having people live in far-away regions if that is not necessary? But it is disadvantageous for the governor whose power and prestige is lost, regardless of whether the governor is elected or appointed.[44]

The governors will prefer an alternative policy of forcing the winner region to subsidize production by diverting some of the primary resource at below the export price (once again, "keeping the lights on"). This adds value to the fictitious capital. And because the subsidy is used to maintain production rather than paid out to the population directly it ties the subsidy to the region rather than to the individual. From the perspective of the governor this is significantly better, as it keeps people in the region and maintains the governor's status. This is a form of addiction through production. By creating opaque production links rather than transparent subsidies governors create more durable forms of transfer that are less immune to political opposition. The obvious point is that subsidies are more efficient if they are individual-specific rather than region-specific. But in the Russian context a "lights on" policy is preferred by both the recipients (the governors of the loser regions) and the donors (Moscow).

"Lights on" versus wage subsidies

The previous section described the mechanism by which a policy of maintaining production and supply chains could ensure that enough of the resource could be diverted to the loser region to keep its factories operating – to keep its lights on. But is that sufficient to prevent migration from the loser regions? Will not the loser region's workers still be attracted by the higher wages that result from reform in the winner regions? The experience of Germany in the 1990s is instructive in this regard.

After the reunification of East and West Germany it was feared that the huge income differentials between the regions would lead to migration *en masse* to the West. The federal government's response was to effectively pay a supplement to the wages of workers in the former East Germany to reduce the wage gap that was assumed to be the driver of migration. Research concluded, however, that the wage supplement did not address the workers' real concern. Surveys cited by Akerlof *et al.* (1990: 46) found that it was not the wage gap but absence of a job that drove migration.

"Wage differentials will not induce them to move, but lack of work for a sufficiently long period will drive them to it." This suggests that for Moscow – the winner region that wants to prevent migration – "lights on" is precisely the efficient policy: it is cheaper than wage supplements, and it works.

Another advantage for Moscow of "lights on" over wage supplements is that the former maintains a key factor that slows migration – liquidity constraints – in place. Wage supplements tend to weaken the liquidity constraints. Andrienko and Guriev (2004) studied migration across Russia's regions and found that liquidity constraints were a major deterrent to migration. Indeed, they found that for the poorest regions – our "loser" regions – an increase in income raised rather than reduced out-migration. Hence, for a winner region intent on preventing in-migration, "lights on" is bound to be preferred to wage subsidies.

Conclusion

We have examined why market-preserving federalism has not worked in Russia. Inefficient regional boundaries combined with the predominance of loser regions rendered federalism ineffective at promoting market development. During the 1990s the inefficiency of federalism in Russia was paramount. With locally elected governors, the owners of fictitious capital had natural allies in their effort to attract the rents they needed to survive. One of Vladimir Putin's first policies upon coming to power was to reduce the independence of governors, primarily by eliminating direct elections. At the same time, his system of rent management by means of a special arrangement with the owners of the resource industries – the oligarchs – has ensured that a stronger central government would not challenge the inherited structure of the economy.

Putin's deal with the oligarchs is a protection racket. The arrangement protects their wealth but at the cost of having to utilize the "lights on" policy, perhaps the single most important mechanism that preserves the legacies from the Soviet period. Putin replaced elected governors in order to prevent collusion between them and the resource producers, but his motivation for choosing to appoint governors was not to overturn federalism and eliminate "lights on." Indeed, his appointed governors are expected to support the "lights on" policy, but without colluding with the resource producers against the center. Putin did not eliminate elected governors to stop the transfer of rents to the regions, but to prevent this transfer from taking place outside his purview. The appointed governors play a critical role in "lights on." Hence, Putin can maintain his protection racket and maintain the "lights on" policy.

Postscript: historical digression

The preceding analysis has shown that, with "lights on," the governors of both winner and loser regions can be happy. This equilibrium is inefficient, but stable. In our model, subsidies undermine the competitive discipline on regional policies imposed by mobility of the factors of production. Essential to the "lights on" equilibrium are impediments to mobility that keep people and capital in place. It is important to understand that constraints to mobility of factors of production is not a new problem in Russia.[45] Indeed, it has been a crucial element of Russian economic development for something like 500 years. It is useful to recall Domar's (1970: 18–19) analysis of the rise of serfdom in Russia, which begins with a summary of the historian Kliuchevsky that goes something like this:

- From about the mid-1400s, Russia fights wars that eventually require a military too big to support by taxes.
- The government solves the problem by assigning land to servitors in exchange for service.
- But the system breaks down after the mid-1500s when peasants start to migrate to newly conquered areas in the east and south-east.
- Under pressure from the serving class, the government steadily restricts peasants' freedom, resulting in serfdom by the mid-1600s.

Domar summarizes (1970: 19):

> The economist would recast Kliuchevsky's account as follows: The servitors tried to live off rents (in one form or another) to be collected from their estates. But the estates could not yield a significant amount of rent for the simple reason that land in Russia was not sufficiently scarce relative to labor, and ironically, was made even less scarce by Russian conquests. The scarce factor of production was not land but labor. Hence it was the ownership of peasants and not of land that could yield an income to the servitors or to any non-working landowning class.

The two essential ingredients for the development of serfdom, according to Domar, are: (1) "a high land/labor ratio" and (2) "the government's determination to create a large class of servitors."

Taking this analysis to the current problem of Russia, our story, then, is that the governors and enterprise directors of low-productivity (cold and remote) regions are the "servitors" of today, their physical capital (manufacturing assets) in those locations is the "land" they received from the state, the workers in those manufacturing plants are the "peasants," and the opportunity to move back west to Moscow and so on is the analogue to the opening up of new and fertile land in the Volga valley in the mid-1500s.[46]

Therefore, a strict analogue would be:

> The workers [peasants] migrate westward to Moscow [eastward], leaving the governors' factories [servitors' land] with a shortage of labor. Under pressure by the governors [servitors], the government restricts the workers' [peasants'] mobility, resulting in continued employment in enterprises in loser regions [serfdom].

But can we really consider loser regions to have high capital–labor ratios? The key point here is to distinguish actual capital and fictitious capital.[47] In loser regions there are enterprises that appear to be capital-intensive (the τ-effect once again). They are actually loss-making, but subsidies and transfers allow them to keep producing. In a virtual sense they have high capital–labor ratios, but if labor were free to leave the regions this would destroy the pretense that these enterprises are productive and that the capital has value.[48] Hence, to maintain the pretense the governors need the labor to stay put.

5 Human capital

Introduction

There are parallels between Russia's physical capital and its human capital. In both cases large stocks of capital were accumulated in the Soviet period, while in the post-Soviet period the existing stocks appear to have deteriorated rapidly at the same time that the rate of new additions to the stock has plummeted. A nation's human capital is typically measured by the number of people in the labor force and their skills (usually expressed as levels of educational attainment and years of work experience). Health status is sometimes added. In today's Russia both population numbers and health status present a picture of a country in crisis. The trends in education appear more positive. But in all three dimensions there is the same issue as we observed for physical capital: Are our measurements correct? Or does Russia's human capital display the same discrepancy between nominal and actual value as its physical capital?

In this chapter we will present data on the quantity and quality of the three components of Russia's human capital mentioned above: population size, education, and health.[1] In addition, we will consider an under-appreciated element of the quality of human capital, namely its geographical location. Even more than physical capital, human capital can be disadvantaged by climate and remoteness. For all of these components we will try to sort out the measurement issues. Finally, we will examine the most critical question of all: What, if any, are the expected returns on investment in each dimension of human capital in Russia? In one important regard, accumulation of human capital differs from accumulation of physical capital. Growth models show clearly that investment rates in physical capital are positively correlated with economic growth. However, it turns out – despite much conventional wisdom to the contrary – that there is no such empirical basis to indicate that for a country at Russia's current development level, investments to increase the size, educational levels, or health of its population can be expected to contribute to faster growth. This fact signals that policies for investment in human capital can be a bear trap: that this is, in other words, an area in which well-meaning efforts to solve what appears to be a problem can be wasted or, worse, lead to slower growth.

We will organize our discussion of Russia's human capital around the following stylized facts relating to the country's demographic and human capital situation:

- *Population size.* The population is shrinking, to a greater extent and for a longer time than almost any other country's today.
- *Age structure.* The working age population is collapsing. The number of young and old people each productive worker will have to support (the "dependency ratio") is going to rise sharply.
- *Fertility.* Birth rates are down.
- *Mortality.* Death rates are up. Not only are they much higher than those of the rest of the world, but they have grown worse over recent decades.
- *Health.* The overall health of the population in all age groups is poor.
- *Education.* The stock of skills is in question. The education system appears to be performing poorly despite high levels of education per worker.
- *Location.* Still too many workers are handicapped because they live in cold and remote areas. The phenomenon of "de-urbanization" is also reported.

Population size

In the 20 years from 1992 through 2011 13.4 million more Russians died than were born.[2] Not even significant net in-migration into Russia from other countries was enough to offset this high net natural loss of population. As a result, Russia since the early 1990s has suffered a huge decline in its population – more than all but eight other countries in the world.[3] From 1993 to 2010 the country lost more people than in the decade during and immediately after World War I and the Bolshevik Revolution. In absolute numbers, the population loss was close to that in World War II (Figure 5.1).

The decline in population has been and remains a politically charged issue. The lack of rigorous scientific findings on the causes of Russia's population loss has allowed politicians to freely assign blame for the population decline as they choose, with communists and other leftists claiming that it was due to ill-considered market reforms in the post-Soviet years, while those on the liberal pro-market side attribute it to the decades-long Soviet legacy.[4] Still, nearly all of Russia's political leaders agree that Russia's shrinking

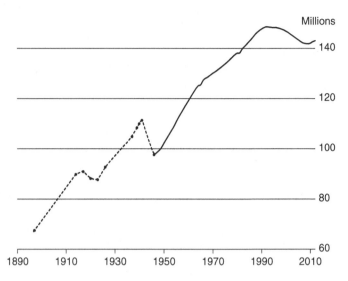

Figure 5.1 Russia's population, 1897–2012

Note: The data are annual from 1946 to the present. The earlier period has several major gaps, in particular 1897–1913, 1926–38, and 1941–6.

population is a threat to the country's economic development and that reversing the negative trend is a policy priority.

In fact, it has become evident in more recent years that some of the most negative scenarios for future population have been exaggerated. As Figure 5.1 shows, Russia's total population grew in 2011. It remains to be seen whether this growth can continue over a longer term, but since 2000 there has been a steady decline in death rates and an increase in birth rates. There was still a net natural loss of population in 2011, but it was the smallest since the beginning of the 1990s (Figure 5.2). Meanwhile, migration continues to be positive (Figure 5.3). Over 1990–2011 total net in-migration into Russia was 5.3 million. Both emigration and immigration were high in the early post-Soviet period, declining subsequently. In the last six years (2006–2011) average out-migration rates have been only 7 percent of what they were in 1990–1995. For the past few years there has been an steady net outflow of about 40,000 a year against an inflow of over 250,000 a year.

The recent positive trends have caused major revisions in some negative projections for the future. A good example is the forecasting of the US Census Bureau. The Census Bureau had for several years, and as recently as 2010, predicted a steady drop in Russia's population to under 110 million by 2050.

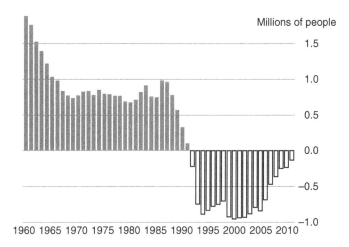

Figure 5.2 Natural population increase/decrease in Russia, 1960–2011

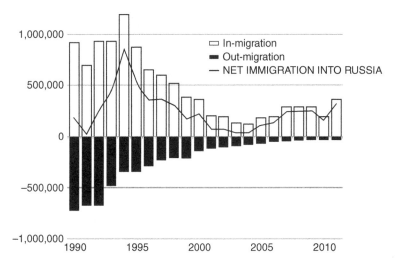

Figure 5.3 Migration into and out of Russia, 1990–2011

Its 2012 forecast, however, revised that figure sharply upward, to 130 million (Figure 5.4). The discrepancy between the forecasts is disconcerting and raises questions about the methodology used. But it also underscores the fallacy of merely projecting current trends into the future without properly appreciating the specific circumstances. Russia's transition shock was a large one, larger than many people had anticipated. But, as in the case of many such large

Millions

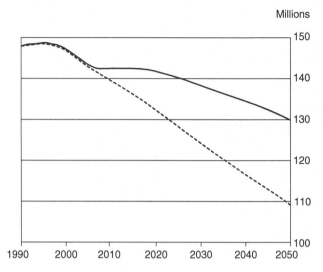

Figure 5.4 US Census Bureau projections of Russia's population to 2050

Note: Dashed line = 2010 projection; solid line = 2012 revised projection.

shocks, it was short-lived. Individuals and families adjust and adapt. They tend to revert to previous patterns of behavior, for better or worse.

Population size and economic growth

Russia's negative population growth has been perhaps the major component of a proclaimed demographic "crisis" in Russia. As we have indicated, the sustained population decrease was extraordinary. We will describe other demographic trends that are even more unusual, sometimes bewilderingly so, but our concern is economics and, no matter how unusual a phenomenon is, we still need to ask, "so what?" How does it matter for economic growth? In the context of this study, to deserve the label of "crisis" the trend in question must be shown to have strong negative consequences for Russia's future economic development.

There is a rather obvious positive correlation between population size and total wealth: big countries tend to be big economically; and Russia fits in precisely where one would expect. Russia is the eighth largest country in the world by both population and total wealth (Figure 5.5).

But is there a relationship between population *growth* and measures of economic performance? A simple scatter plot (Figure 5.6) of countries' population growth rates and GDP growth rates measured over the period 1970–2008 shows a negative correlation: the slower a country's population

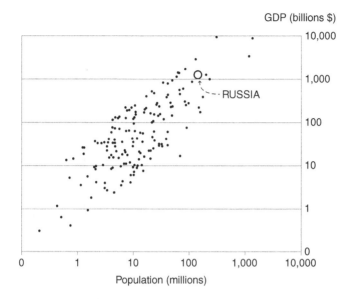

GDP (billions $)

Figure 5.5 Population and GDP levels across 161 countries

Note: GDP is for 2008, PPP-adjusted and measured in 1990 Geary-Khamis dollars. Population is mid-year 2008.

Source: Angus Maddison, "Statistics on World Population, GDP and Per Capita GDP, 1–2008 AD" available at: http://www.ggdc.net/MADDISON/oriindex.htm.

growth, the faster its per capita GDP growth. This follows, of course, from the neoclassical growth model, where the steady state capital–labor ratio and the level of per-capita income are inversely related to the population growth rate. The results of the growth regressions we reported in Chapter 2 – the Levine–Renelt equation and our own preferred version – gave empirical support to this prediction. Recall that the coefficient on population growth was negative in both cases. Hence, if the population growth rate increased, all else equal, one would expect per-capita income to fall in the transition to the new steady state.

The bottom line is that while concerns about population size and population growth may be important for the exponents of Great Power thinking in Russia today, there is no reason to think that the country needs to have a growing population if its main goal is economic welfare.[5] In fact, efforts targeted at promoting population growth as a goal in itself may be at odds with the goal of increasing individual wealth and welfare over the longer term. In other words, it is a bear trap.

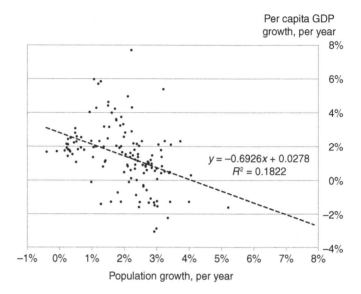

Figure 5.6 Population growth versus per-capita GDP growth, 161 countries,
1970–2008

Age structure

There are several concerns about the age structure of Russia's population
that are worth consideration. One is that Russia's working age population is expected to shrink at a faster rate than the overall population (see
Figure 5.7).

Another age-structure concern is the cohort of women of child-bearing
age. The number of babies born in the future depends on the number of
women capable of giving birth as well as the number of children each
one is likely to bear (fertility rate). If the most recent forecasts of Russia's
population made by the US Census Bureau are borne out, it is apparent that
births will decline. Those forecasts show the cohort of women aged 16–39
decreasing by 27 percent by 2030 (Figure 5.8).

A third widely discussed age-structure concern is the number of 18-year-
old males, since these represent the pool of draft-age men. Ten years ago
Russia had more 18-year-olds than ever before in its history, but within
the next five years that number may drop to the lowest in over 120 years
(Figure 5.9). Adding to the issue is the ethno-cultural composition of the
draft pool (there is a growing share of Muslims). These prospects have led
to proposals to expand the pool of draft-eligible men by extending the age

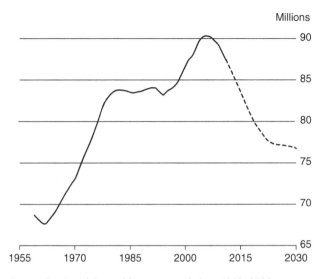

Figure 5.7 Russia's working age population, 1959–2030

Note: Russian legislated definition of working age: 16–59 for men and 16–54 for women.

Source: Historical data and forecast from GKS, medium variant.

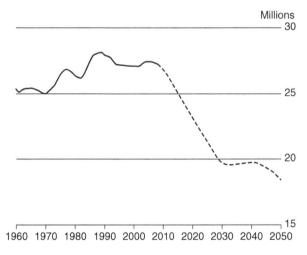

Figure 5.8 Number of women of childbearing age (15–39) in Russia, actual and projected

Source: Historical data from GKS, forecasts from US Census Bureau, 2012 International Database (IDB).

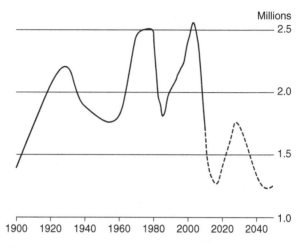

Figure 5.9 Number of 18-year-olds in Russia, 1900–2050

Note: For reasons of availability of historical data on age cohorts by gender, the data shown in the figure are for both males and females.

Source: Historical data from GKS, forecasts from US Census Bureau, 2012 International Database (IDB).

of selection for service to 30. Were such a measure to be implemented it would, of course, further reduce the number of working age males in the civilian labor force.

All this said, the most important aspect of the age structure of the population is the ratio of the members of the population not in the labor force to the productive members of the population (those active in the labor force). This is the dependency ratio. When the dependency ratio is low economies experience a "demographic dividend," as savings per-capita will be higher. When the dependency ratio rises, growth prospects deteriorate, as the same pool of workers must support a larger pool of young and old.[6] The picture of past, present, and future dependency ratios for Russia is given in Figure 5.10,[7] which shows that, for all the negative demographic trends Russia has experienced over the past 20 years, it has moved in a favorable direction as regards its dependency ratio. That is, the productive part of the population has seen its burden steadily reduced throughout this period. However, the burden is now about to rise steeply.

Figure 5.11 shows how the picture for Russia compares with that for a number of other countries. Several observations can be made. First, Russia's current dependency ratio is quite low relative to the other countries, even going back to the 1930s. Second, the projected steep rise in its ratio over

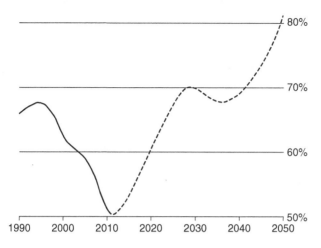

Figure 5.10 Dependency ratios for Russia, 1990–2050

Note: Dependency ratio = (old + young)/working age, where old = 65+,
young = 0–15, and working age = 16–64.

Source: Historical data from GKS, forecasts from US Census Bureau, 2012
International Database (IDB).

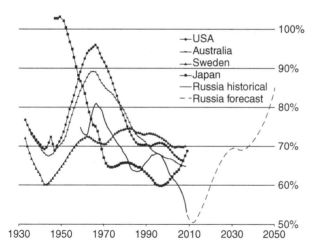

Figure 5.11 Historical dependency ratios in selected countries and forecasts
for Russia

Note: Dependency ratio = (old + young)/working age, where old = 65+, young = 0–15,
and working age = 16–64.

Source: Historical data from GKS, forecasts from US Census Bureau, 2012
International Database (IDB).

the next 20 years will bring it only to the same level as the others are today. Third, even if it were to continue to rise as shown until 2050 Russia would not be entering totally uncharted territory. In the past Japan, the United States, and Australia have had dependency ratios as high.

It is important to note that countries may differ among one another and over time in how the dependency ratio is composed. The burden part – the numerator of the ratio – is the sum of young and old. Eberstadt (2010) points out that the old in all societies consume more than the young and that, therefore, they represent a greater burden. This trend is likely to become even stronger with improvements in medical care, which focus expenditure on the last years of an extending life span. A breakdown of the aggregate dependency ratio into separate ratios for young and old is therefore instructive.

The data in Table 5.1 (along with Figure 5.11) show that in these scenarios of population dynamics it would not be until 2030 that Russia's dependency ratios reached those of other developed countries today. By 2050, if the forecasts are accurate, Russia would have an extraordinarily high ratio of "Old/WA" – in other words, a heavy burden of older citizens on the active labor force. This burden can be eased if more of the old remain in the labor force.

Mortality

Russia's high death rates have been the most anomalous of all the demographic trends examined here. Figure 5.12 shows that deaths per 1,000 population rose almost continuously in Russia from the early 1960s

Table 5.1 Decomposition of dependency ratios

	$\dfrac{Young}{WA}$	$\dfrac{Old}{WA}$	$\dfrac{Old+Young}{WA}$
Sweden (2008)	40%	30%	70%
Japan (2009)	31%	38%	69%
USA (2007)	46%	21%	67%
Russia (2009)	33%	20%	53%
Russia (2030)	36%	34%	70%
Russia (2050)	35%	46%	81%

Note: Young = ages 0–19; old = 65 and over; WA (working age) = 20–64. Historical data from the Human Mortality Database (www.mortality.org). The figures for Russia for 2030 and 2050 are based on population projections by the US Census Bureau, 2012.

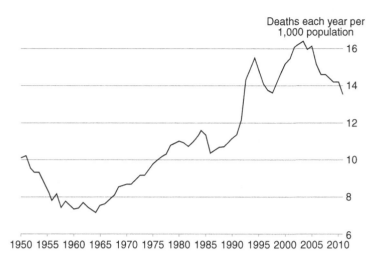

Figure 5.12 Death rates in Russia, 1950–2011

until the mid-1990s – a stark contrast with Western Europe and most other industrialized countries. Only a brief period in the mid-1980s interrupted the negative trend. The break occurred in the initial years (1985–6) of Mikhail Gorbachev's anti-alcohol campaign, but thereafter the rise in death rates resumed and continued through 1995. Since then the picture has been mixed. The death rates for the entire population have declined for the past 7–8 years, but they still remain some 80 percent higher than they were a half century ago.

Male mortality is particularly alarming. Russian males of prime working age – the 25–55 age range – die at rates 4 to 4.5 times higher than Americans and 7 to 11 times higher than Swedes. The gap between Russia and advanced Western countries is widest for young adult males. The last time Sweden, for instance, had a death rate as high as Russia's today for its 30–34-year-olds was 1876 (except for the single year of the 1918 epidemic). Russian 26-year-old men today die at the same rate as Swedish 56-year-olds.

A comparison of Russia's male death rates today with those in 1960 (Figure 5.13) shows that it is among only very young cohorts that mortality has declined. Males as young as 16 die at higher rates now than they did in 1960. The increase in mortality has been highest for men between the ages of 35 and 50: they die at rates double those of 1960.

The reasons for the high mortality are surely complicated.[8] Lifestyle choices play a key role. All too many Russian men are drinking themselves to death.[9] Smoking, shown in a recent study to be comparable in effect to

Figure 5.13 Ratio of male death rates in Russia, 2000–05 average, to 1960, by age cohort.

Note: Values <1.0 signify improvement (a lowering of death rates) compared to 1960; values >1.0 signify a deterioration.

Source: Human Mortality Database, www.mortality.org.

drinking, is another factor. Whatever the causes, the deaths of so many men of these ages represents a significant loss of Russia's potential labor force. One way to gauge how big the loss is would be to take a country such as Sweden as a benchmark and calculate how many potential working years are lost in aggregate owing to excess deaths (the excess of Russia's age-specific death rates for males and females over Sweden's). We include the other so-called BRIC countries (Brazil, India, and China) for further reference. As Figure 5.14 shows, Russia is losing some 18 percent of working years for men compared to less than 3 percent for Sweden. This is quite a dramatic difference.

If measures could be taken to reduce excess deaths among working age men and women, that would, of course, expand the pool of productive workers and could help compensate for the declining size of birth cohorts in the future. On the other hand, the effect on the dependency ratio is less clear. An improvement in survival rates among those of working age will almost certainly be accompanied by an improvement for those of older ages as well. Therefore the ratio of persons above working age to those still in the labor force (the ratio *Old/WA* in Table 5.1) might not change.[10] Recall from Table 5.1 that Russia's ratio of *Old/WA* today is 0.20 compared to Sweden's

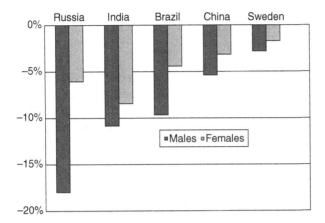

Figure 5.14 Potential working years lost by deaths in 15–65 age range (percent of maximum)

Source: Authors' calculations from data for 2006 from World Health Organization, "Life Tables for WHO Member States, 2006." http://www.who.int/healthinfo/statistics/mortality_life_tables/en/.

0.30, thanks to the fact that greater numbers of Swedes survive into older age. Policies that move Russia towards a "Swedish" survival pattern might increase the demographic burden.

If, then, improved survival does not lead to lower dependency ratios, it is clear that the only way to raise per-capita wealth for the entire population is to make each working age person more productive. This brings us back to the economic growth exercise. In particular, we must move beyond mere numbers of workers to consider the other attributes of human capital, those that reflect quality: health, education, and location. These are considered in the next three sections.

Health[11]

Can improved health enhance economic growth through its impact on human capital? To many, the answer to this question is a self-evident "yes." The logic is summed up in the introductory section of a recent volume entitled *Health and Economic Growth* (Lopez-Casanovas *et al.* 2005: 3):

> Good health raises levels of human capital, and this has a positive effect on individual productivity and on economic growth rates. Better health increases workforce productivity by reducing incapacity, debility, and

the number of days lost to sick leave, and increases the opportunities an individual has of obtaining better paid work. Further, good health helps to forge improved levels of education by increasing levels of schooling and scholastic performance.

In fact, however, the evidence for the effects of health on economic growth is mixed. The sticking point is that while better health might lead to greater productivity on the part of the individual worker (following the apparently obvious line of argument presented in the quote above), the overall societal effect can be different. For one thing, better health usually means better survival rates for the dependent part of the population. Therefore, the greater wealth produced by the individually more productive worker has to be shared among more dependents. There is also the capital dilution argument: as more workers survive, a given stock of physical capital is shared among more workers, so the capital–labor ratio falls.

Research on the contribution of good health to economic growth in the 1990s and early 2000s seemed to show that health has a strong positive impact on economic growth, at least for developing countries (and over the long period of Western economic development). At the macro level there is no question of a correlation between health and wealth. There is an important question of causality, however. Does health promote wealth, or does wealth lead to better health? Or are both the result of unmeasured third factors? A number of more recent studies argue that improved health leads to little, no, or even negative results for economic growth (Acemoglu and Johnson 2007; Ashraf *et al.* 2008; Weil 2007).

Most of the data used to estimate the health–growth linkage have been drawn from developing countries. The reason for this is straightforward: the variation in both health outcomes and growth performance is higher among these countries, so the effects should be easier to tease out in this setting. Yet, even with these data, it is hard to find a statistically significant effect. Bhargava *et al.* (2001) used a cross section of poor and rich countries and found a positive effect of increased adult survival rates (ASRs) on GDP growth rates for the entire sample. But the magnitude of this effect was quite small, even for the poorest countries: a 1 percentage point increase in the ASR was associated with a 0.014 percentage point increase in the growth rate. In other words, increasing the ASR from, say, 40 percent to 60 percent – a huge improvement – would only result in an extra 0.28 percentage points of annual growth. More important for our analysis, Bhargava *et al.* concluded that the positive effects of an increase in the ASR on economic growth rates *disappeared entirely for richer countries*. For countries at Russia's current level of per-capita GDP the net effect of raising the survival ratio was *negative*.[12]

Even if the cross-country evidence (contra Bhargava *et al.* 2001) had shown a positive effect at Russia's level of per-capita income, there is a real question over whether the effect could be transferred to Russia, as Russia's current level of per-capita income is already quite high compared to its level of health. Consider its position on a scatter plot of ASRs versus per-capita national income as in Figure 5.15. Russia is a huge outlier, being richer than its current level of health would predict. Alternatively, one could conclude that, given its current level of per-capita income, Russia should have a much higher ASR. The most likely reason for this outcome is that Russia's resource wealth has given it a per-capita income considerably greater than its social capital would suggest. This suggests that improving Russia's health would have little, if any, impact on GDP per capita.[13]

In sum, as counter-intuitive as it may seem, there is no evidence that Russia's growth prospects are impaired by its abysmal health performance. Hence, we conclude that improving health is not a silver bullet for ensuring Russia's future economic growth. Health investment is properly treated not as investment at all but as consumption. Virtually everyone would agree that "[g]ood health is a crucial component of overall well-being" (Lopez-Casanovas *et al.* 2005: 3). While it almost certainly can (should) be justified to spend money to improve citizens' health for welfare or humanitarian reasons, it would be a mistake to assume that this is an investment that will "pay for itself" by contributing to more economic

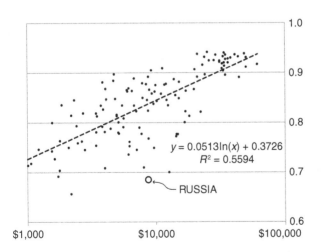

Figure 5.15 Adult survival ratio versus per-capita national income
(134 countries. Survival rate on *y*-axis, income on *x*-axis)

Note: ASR (adult survival rate) = probability of dying (per 1,000 population) between 15 and 60, both sexes, 2006. GNI (gross national income) per capita (PPP international $), 2006.

growth. Russia could spend great amounts on preventive and curative health care, enlightenment, and so on, and succeed in reducing deaths, and yet find that economic performance fails to improve at all because the factors that led to high mortality are still there, and it is those factors, not the mortality *per se*, that was causing bad performance.

Education

The one component of human capital that is most often regarded as investment is education. Society as a whole, and individuals, seek to enhance the stock of human capital by devoting time and money to the acquisition of new knowledge and skills through schooling. As in the case of physical capital investment, human capital investment is assumed to be appropriate to the demands of the market. Normally, there is no concern that measuring the stock of human capital by accumulated investments will lead to systematic errors. Human capital is a stock of "skills," and those skills are typically measured by years of education. Normally, we do not worry that a country will accumulate "the wrong education" on a systematic scale. However, in the Russian case this is an important consideration, as the Soviet economy demanded a different kind of education stock, one appropriate for a planned economy. One might assume that the continued production of "Soviet" human capital would not persist after the demise of the Soviet economy. But this has not been the case. As we shall explain, the forces that preserve legacies in relation to physical capital operate in a similar, if not stronger, manner with regard to human capital. Hence, the education investments currently being made at both the public and private level are being overvalued.

By many nominal measures of accumulation of educational human capital, Russia leads the world. What is striking is that so many of its citizens have completed secondary education and have entered higher education. A report by the OECD shows that Russia ranks higher than 29 of 34 OECD countries by percentage of the population of ages 25–64 that has completed upper secondary school, and ranks higher than all OECD countries by the percentage of that age group with higher education attainments. Its percentage for the higher education attainment measure is an astounding 54 percent – twice the average for the European Union countries.[14]

At the same time, when it comes to resources devoted to education, whether measured in absolute amounts or as a share of GDP or budget, the picture is quite different. In terms of the amount spent on all educational institutions as a percentage of GDP Russia ranks lower than all but one reporting OECD country (Slovakia), and in terms of spending per student at all educational levels in absolute amounts (measured for all countries in US dollars at purchasing power parity exchange rates) Russia outranked only Chile, Mexico, and Slovakia in the OECD. In terms of higher education spending per student, only Slovakia was lower. Figure 5.16 shows how Russia's spending on higher education compares with selected OECD countries.

The contrast between Russia's educational attainment rates and its modest spending might suggest that Russia has done a remarkable job of accumulating educational capital for a relatively small financial investment. However, a closer examination of some measures of the quality of Russian education tells a different story. Since 2000 the OECD has conducted a special program – the Programme for International Student Assessment, or PISA – to judge the quality of school systems throughout the world. PISA assessments are held every three years, with each round assessing student performance in reading, mathematics, and science.[15] In the 2009 assessment Russia ranked lower than 29 of 34 OECD countries in both math and science. Only Chile and Mexico had students with lower reading scores

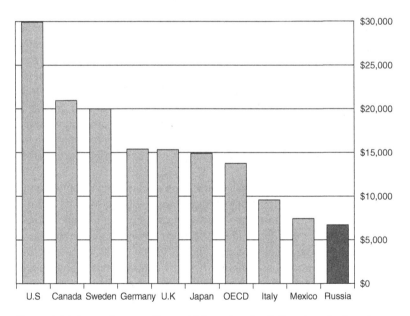

Figure 5.16 Per student spending on higher education in Russia and selected OECD countries in 2008 in USD, converted from national currencies at PPP exchange rates

Source: OECD *Education at a Glance 2011*. Table B1.1a. "Annual expenditure per student by educational institutions for all services (2008)."

than Russia. Russian youths' poor performance in subjects compared with those from other countries in the PISA study calls into question the value of the nominal educational capital it reports. PISA shows that in general, in education, you get what you pay for. Russia ranks where it would be expected to by spending, not by nominal attainment. Russia is not paying much, and it is not getting much.[16]

There is no analogue to the PISA assessments for higher educational performance. A poor proxy are the rankings of higher education institutions worldwide, of which three are widely cited. They all show the remarkably poor performance of even those Russian universities deemed to be of flagship status. The Academic Ranking of World Universities (ARWU), often referred to as the Shanghai Ranking, ranks only one Russian university in its top 400; the Times Higher Education World University Rankings ranks two Russian institutions in its top 400; and the QS Top University Ranking includes five.[17]

Given all these findings, the question then is: What is the real value of Russia's educational human capital? Clearly, some sort of discount factor ought to be applied to correct for what according to all evidence seems to be an overstatement of national human capital measured by, say, years of schooling per capita or per member of the labor force. A more complicated issue is to determine to what extent the human capital represented by years of education is suited to the challenges of the economy. "Appropriateness" is an important concept. Human capital enhances productivity if it is complementary to physical capital. To the extent that human capital is inappropriate for what is needed, it will contribute less to production. In the case of Russia the type of education that might have been the right one for the Soviet system, with its incentives, might well not be right for a market economy.

Another question is that of the distribution of educational capital in the population, in terms not just of years of schooling but also of its quality. The PISA results, for instance, are averages for the entire population. We know that there is great inequality in many other indicators, such as health, life expectancy, income, and so on, and it is likely that this carries over to educational quality. Perhaps extraordinarily high levels for some substantial part of the population are being pulled down by very low levels among others. The issue for productivity is, then, whether having a population that is moderately well educated across the board is better than having one that may be generally less well educated but has a pool of superstars. To put it differently, which is better for growth: to raise the average level of education of the population or to produce a critical mass of Sergey Brins?[18] Growth theory has not, as of yet, dealt with the distribution of human capital, and there do not appear to be any empirical studies that answer that question either. There may be other considerations – equity, for instance – for desiring broad-based educational improvement. These may lead to increased welfare and to the sustainability of democracy. But there is little evidence that these factors affect a country's long-term growth potential, despite what may seem to be an intuitive connection.

There is one important difference between mismeasured human capital and mismeasured physical capital. Mismeasured physical capital means that less is returned for a given level of sacrifice. It means that you have actually invested less than you thought, and that more sacrifice is needed to get what you expected to earn. In the case of human capital the problem is different. Here it is a question not just of the *level* but also of the *type*. With misallocated human capital more is not a solution. Two humanities PhDs cannot substitute for an accountant.[19]

In general, however, one could conclude that for an economy with a tightening supply of labor, as Russia appears to be becoming, education programs that maximize the ability to adapt, to change occupational track, may be more important than absolute levels of an education that is suited only to specific technologies. Indeed, if having a higher level of specialized education makes individuals less likely to "re-tool" themselves for a new occupation, it may be the case that more education is worse, not better. The argument here is consistent with the notion of addiction.[20] A dinosaur factory inherited from the Soviet Union commands rents precisely because it represents so much sunk investment. This is investment not only in physical capital – the machines, buildings, and so on – but also in human capital, including education. In fact, the argument for allotting more rents to the Soviet-era dinosaur factories is strengthened by the argument that "the workers cannot move, and they cannot change occupation." The more that has been spent to develop the current structure, the greater the claim for future rents. For both physical capital and educational human capital, addiction is based on ignoring the dictum that sunk costs are sunk.

Location

We examined the general problem of mislocation of factors of production in Chapter 3. The temperature per capita (TPC) index we introduced in that chapter was intended to give us a crude instrument to estimate the extent of mismeasurement (the τ factor) that might be attributed to the spatial misallocation of Russia's capital. The TPC applies to human capital as well as physical capital. (In fact, of course, the TPC is a measure of human population in different regions, because population was used as a proxy for all economic activity.) Suppose that we studied Russian economic growth using a human capital augmented production function, say of the form:

$$y_t = K_t^{\alpha} H_t^{\beta} (A_t L_t)^{1-\alpha-\beta} \tag{5.1}$$

where $\alpha, \beta \in [0,1]$, $\alpha + \beta \in [0,1]$, and t denotes time. Here K and H are physical and human capital respectively, and AL is productivity-augmented labor. If we measure the contributions to growth with this model, and if human capital is being overmeasured, then we will attribute inferior economic outcomes to low productivity. Just as we argued that $\tau < 1$ ought to be applied as a discount factor to K to control for mismeasurement of physical capital, we require a similar factor for human capital. We would have something of the form:

$$y_t = \tau_K K_t^{\alpha} \tau_H H_t^{\beta} (A_t L_t)^{1-\alpha-\beta} \tag{5.2}$$

where $\tau_K, \tau_H \in [0,1]$ are the respective discount factors to offset the impact of spatial and legacy effects on the measurement of asset stocks (physical and human) in Russia. Just as we argued with respect to physical capital, ignoring these discount factors attributes to much of Russia's inadequate growth performance to low TFP, and not enough to the lack of effective inputs.[21]

It is important to note that there are two fundamental causes for $\tau_H < 1$ in Russia. One key factor is the spatial legacy. Russia's *effective* human capital is less than measured because much of it is located in the wrong place. This is similar to problems we identified with physical capital. But in the case of human capital a more important factor is type: the inherited capital stock is ill-suited to the needs of the market economy.

De-urbanization?

One further alleged negative demographic trend in Russia deserves comment. There has been some discussion that "Russia is becoming de-urbanized" (notably, Eberstadt 2010: 26ff). According to aggregate statistics the trend would appear indisputable. Between 1991 and 2009 Russia's official statistics show a decline in the share of the population classified as urban in 42 of the country's 78 regions. In the country as a whole the urban share declined from 73.8 percent to 73.1 percent. However, it turns out that this decline reflects changes in the definition of urban versus rural – changes apparently implemented unevenly and inconsistently throughout the country.[22] The statistical decline did not, in fact, reflect a shift of population out of cities to the countryside.

A more significant means of measuring urbanization or de-urbanization in the Russian context would be the population dynamics of large cities.

The group of cities that had a population of over half a million in 1991 (a total of 33) has on net gained population in absolute terms since then. Admittedly, most of the gain was due to Moscow. If Moscow is excluded from the analysis, these large cities did show a modest loss in population (–1.8 percent in total over 18 years). But that is a substantially slower rate than Russia's overall population loss in the period (–4.4 percent). That means that Russia did not "de-urbanize" in this sense. Relatively speaking, Russia urbanized by 7.8 percent between 1991 and 2009.

But of course the real problem is that some of this urban growth was in cities that should not have grown. In one sense Russia does need to "de-urbanize," but selectively. That is, it needs to shrink cities that are mislocated. Moscow is the bright spot, but it should be even brighter. When cities such as Novosibirsk, Omsk, and Perm lose population, it is nothing to lament. They are far larger than they by rights should be.

Conclusion

Let us summarize the findings of this chapter on Russia's human capital. Human capital is multi-dimensional. By examining each dimension – population numbers, age structure, health, education, and location – we have been able to identify several of them as potential bear traps. These are areas where money spent with the intention of promoting growth may actually end up having negative effects on growth. First, efforts to promote population growth will not contribute to economic growth. Decreasing death rates can help expand the labor force, but since they may likely increase rather than decrease the dependency ratio, they will hamper growth. Similarly, improved population health will not be growth-enhancing (although it will raise welfare). What are *not* bear traps are, first, efforts to shift the location of the population to warmer and less remote regions and, second, proper measures to improve education. Fixing Russia's education problems requires fixing education policy. The current educational system limits mobility and so helps to preserve structural and spatial misallocation within the economy as a whole: it is more geared to produce young people for loser regions than a reformed educational system would be. A better educational system would enhance labor mobility and would make it hard to keep labor in the loser regions, because graduates would want to locate in the winner regions. It should not be a surprise that industrial feudalists would support the current educational system and in fact would seek to make it more like the Soviet system, as it helps to produce more claims for addiction. Each new miseducated young person is a 40-year claim on resources for a loser region. This is what makes failure to reform the education system in Russia so costly. It also explains why there are such strong vested interests involved in preventing reform.

6 Conclusion

In this book we have analyzed the potential barriers to Russia's long-term growth and the mistaken policy directions that might result from misunderstanding those obstacles. Our argument throughout has been that it is easy to misdiagnose the sources of Russia's difficulties. At one level, the issues are obvious. The Russian economy is less efficient than it should be, its market institutions are less effective than they can be, and its political economy less capable of responding to Russia's long-term challenges than it should be. These constitute the "typical set" of Russia's problems, and it is easy to collect information about them. Russia always fares very low in corruption rankings (taking high as good). The weaknesses in property rights enforcement are notorious. A focus on the "typical set" makes it seem that these problems can simply be overturned with sufficient will. But they stem from deeper causes. They are the outgrowth of specific Russian institutions that help preserve a legacy of misallocation. They preserve the poor location choices and poor use of assets that are endemic in Russia. This makes the inferior equilibrium self-reinforcing. Russia's bad institutions sustain the misallocations, and its resource wealth makes this feasible.

The question arises, however: Will not time weaken these factors sufficiently to allow a new modernized economy to appear and eventually dominate?[1] Can the passage of time and a focus on modernization eventually overtake the bear traps? Will efforts to promote modernization and innovation – like Skolkovo – lead to a new Russian economy?[2] While the dream of "Skolkovization" might have always been fantasy, recent events make it clear that this road now has insurmountable political hurdles. Since the fall of 2011, in the lead-up to the Duma and presidential elections of the winter and spring and the aftermath of those elections in the form of public protests against the leadership and the "Putin system," political considerations have weighed more heavily on economic policy decisions from the top. Before, in his management of the Russian economy, Vladimir Putin's focus was on a narrow group of individuals – the so-called oligarchs – with whom he interacted in an informal contractual arrangement that we have in other work termed Putin's Protection Racket (Gaddy and Ickes 2009; 2010; 2011). Under the arrangement, Putin would protect the oligarchs' ownership of their assets (mainly in the resource sectors) provided they shared the resource rent with the value-subtracting manufacturing sectors.[3] This system worked remarkably well to preserve social and political stability throughout Putin's tenure as leader of Russia, but the demonstrations in Moscow showed that there is another source of political instability that rent-sharing and the Protection Racket cannot cope with. The new "creative class" – so far heavily concentrated in Moscow – is independent of and in opposition to the old dinosaur sectors and their regions.

Putin's dilemma is that he needs Russia to modernize, but policies to promote a new economy based on innovation and independent thinking will unavoidably strengthen the new social strata, making the Moscow problem worse. Rent-sharing cannot solve the Moscow problem; indeed, since the distribution of rent to the regions is in effect a tax on Moscow, it will only intensify Moscow's discontent. The public protests undermine Putin's legitimacy. Yet a precondition for the oligarchs to stick to their contract with Putin is that he is the undisputed ruler of the country and in full control of its various mechanisms of enforcement and repression (in no small part so he can protect them from expropriation or excessive taxation of their wealth). For this reason, a "Skolkovo" that is truly independent is politically impermissible.[4] In Putin's eyes, a Moscow that grows by expanding its creative class is a threat in itself. The risk that it might constitute a model for other regions is even more dangerous.

Putin's response to the dilemma has been to try to co-opt the innovation initiative. His offensive is defense modernization, with Skolkovo's results being channeled into the defense sector. Skolkovo will be dependent on Putin. New "Skolkovos" will be set up in the regions and attached directly to defense conglomerates. Meanwhile, Putin is putting more funding directly into the defense plants. His ten-year defense modernization plan calls for 23 trillion rubles ($750 billion) to the defense industrial sector.[5] This is all consistent with what appears to be a bigger plan to preserve and expand his own version of the "creative class" – scientists, engineers, skilled workers, and so on –as a counterweight to the protesters in Moscow.[6] Plans to expand population in Siberia and Far East are also part of this.

This strategy has two clear benefits for Putin. First, it counters the attraction of Moscow to the young and slows the growth of the opposition forces that he cannot control. It educates youth in his system, and it gives him a chance to win over the scientists and other members of the intelligentsia that he had seemingly lost over election fraud. Second, it creates a new dependency in the regions. New jobs and incomes are created that are based solely on his ability to channel rents, formal and informal, to the defense modernization program. The whole system is dependent on the rent-sharing enforced through the protection racket with the oligarchs.

The bottom line is that Putin has now adopted a centralized version of "lights on." As we modeled it originally in Chapter 4, "lights on" was a tax on Moscow to support production in the loser regions and thus prevent out-migration of their population to Moscow. But that was a self-imposed tax by Moscow, borne out of the local Moscow concern to avoid congestion costs. Putin's centralized "lights on" policy is, too, a tax on Moscow, but it is one motivated not by Moscow's interests but by Putin's concern to restrain and counter Moscow's weight in politics and policy.

Moscow is an inherent threat to Putin's system because Moscow represents modernization. To return to our opening analogy of the privatization lottery, Moscow is the region that perceives that it does not depend on Putin's restoring the value of losing lottery tickets. It is not dependent on him in the way that the regions are and can thus resist his authority and demand reforms. Putin is trying to modernize Russia without further empowering the citizens of Moscow. All the correct principles for growth that we have identified in this text, the ones that avoid the bear traps – freedom of movement of factors, flexibility and adaptability, and independent decision-making – represent the values of the creative class and are therefore anathema to Putin for *political* reasons.

Putin has bet all his chips on a policy of centralized control of "lights on" with an anti-Moscow emphasis, using the pro-defense industry initiative as a counter to Moscow. The centralized "lights on" policy rules out Skolkovization, and it means that any "normal" reform is off the table. But does it rule out all modernization for Russia? Does it mean there is no future for Russia? This is too pessimistic a conclusion. We believe that there is a sustainable path to a modern Russia. But a sustainable path must be feasible: that is, it must be a solution to the problem given the Russian constraints. We have been arguing throughout this book that the future cannot be considered if the legacies are ignored. We also have to recognize that the Soviet legacies that we have been analyzing place constraints on the set of feasible policies that can be adopted. Hence, our analysis of this potential path of escape is predicated on thinking about what is feasible.

We have already explained how reforms that are thought of in terms of diversification away from oil and gas cannot work for bear trap reasons. Such reforms are, in other words, economically unfeasible.[7] Policies that build on Russia's natural resource advantage, in contrast, are imminently feasible in an economic sense. We argue, therefore, that Russia could embrace resource dependence. We refer to this as the resource track – adopting a set of feasible policy measures that exploit Russia's comparative advantage.

The resource track can avoid bear traps because resources in a cold climate can be exploited efficiently, as is done in Canada. With modern technology there is no reason to locate large population centers in remote regions in order to exploit abundant natural resources.

One might object that a resource focus only deepens the addiction to rents that so contributes to maintaining the Soviet structural legacy we have argued is at the heart of Russia's problems. There is, of course, always the risk that greater availability of the addictive substance – oil and gas rents – leads to deeper addiction, but the process is not automatic. Recall that Russia's addiction is rent-sharing through production in the dinosaur manufacturing sectors. A focus on modernizing the resource industries can offer a built-in resistance to addiction simply because it involves a choice to invest in oil and gas instead of manufacturing. And given the investment requirements necessary to exploit Russia's resource reserves in Eastern Siberia there is a potent and valuable use for the rents that might otherwise go to addicts. If Putin commits to the resource track then intensifying addiction need not occur.

The key difference between defense modernization and the resource track is that the former taxes the sources of growth, while the latter encourages and enhances them. Historical examples from other resource abundant economies show that industries devoted to and based on production from the resource sector can be engines of growth.[8] The resource track is not, by itself, a guarantee of ending addiction, but it does offer the possibility of channeling resource rents away from dinosaur sectors. This is in contrast to defense modernization, which intensifies addiction.

The resource track is feasible economically. Is it feasible politically? We believe so. First, and most important for any policy in Putin's Russia, the resource track does not threaten the current rent management system – that is, Putin's Protection Racket and rent-sharing. Second, the resource track does not represent a capitulation or even a tilt towards Moscow. Placing the emphasis on resources is not a Moscow-centric policy, and it does not carry with it the risk of further empowering Moscow. It is a strategy focused geographically on the regions and socially on the workers. So, for both these reasons, it should be acceptable to Putin.

What, then, might be a possible political scenario to implement the resource track? There are assuredly various options, but, given Putin's current emphasis on national security and national prestige arguments, we suggest that the key step needed to make any policy in Russia today truly feasible politically is to frame it in those terms. Thus, oil and gas have to be defined as the ultimate strategic sectors for the nation, more important even than military defense. That argument has to be made powerfully enough to justify rechanneling the hundreds of billions of dollars now promised to defense away from military "modernization" and towards energy. Once the priority of oil and gas has been established as the political line the government can then proceed with policies to accumulate the physical and human capital needed to support it. Investments in technology, education, and infrastructure can then make sense, because these investments will be made with regard to Russia's economic advantages, not its handicaps. The road to sustainable growth, a road free of bear traps, will lie open.

Notes

Introduction

1 The problem is the difference between growth in real national income and growth in real GDP. When an economy experiences a positive price shock to its exports (resource boom) the real income of exporters rises even though the real output of the resource sector does not. Hence, real national income grows. Real GDP grows too, but only through indirect effects that work through the non-resource sectors of GDP.

2 This point has been recognized in a few studies of resource exporters but has usually been ignored in most growth analyses. For example, it is known that measured aggregate TFP growth for oil exporters is negative, while TFP growth in non-oil sectors in those economies is positive.

3 This is related to the notion of input homogeneity in growth accounting. If labor and capital inputs are taken as homogeneous, then most of US economic growth, for example, can be explained by growth in TFP. But if inputs are heterogeneous, then improvements in the quality of inputs show up as TFP growth when capital and labor are treated as homogeneous. But higher quality capital is really *more* capital, and when this is taken into account, the relative contributions of capital and labor growth versus TFP growth are reversed (see Jorgenson 1990: 23–4). Our argument concerning τ-effects is closely related, but reversed. Now the heterogeneity involves not quality improvements but the barriers imposed by Soviet legacies that diminish the effective quantity of capital and labor inputs.

4 This is also related to the willingness to write down debts. In Japan worthless debts remain on the books and the debt overhang prevents growth. In the US, after the S&L crisis, debts were written off. The lingering effects of the debt overhang were much smaller in the US.

5 Nothing illustrates the problem better than this story ("Vekselberg to Revive Soviet Oil Plant to Save Town") from Bloomberg, May 26, 2010. "Russian billionaire Viktor Vekselberg plans to renovate a moneylosing, Soviet-era synthetic oil plant as President Dmitry Medvedev demands the rich invest in towns left impoverished by dying industries." The largest oil producer in the world will make synthetic oil to save a dying one-plant town. According to a

spokesman for Vekselberg: "While the Zavod Slantsy plant is the only hope for the town's economy, the potential for 'innovation and efficiency' sparked Vekselberg's interest.... [Vekselberg] aims to upgrade the plant and produce synthetic fuel that can compete with petroleum...".

1 Historical prelude

1   See Gaddy and Ickes (2013) for an analysis of Russian resource rents.
2   We have used this metaphor before in *Russia's Virtual Economy* (Gaddy and Ickes 2002).

2 Investment and physical capital

1   The concept of "distance to market" as a way to describe and analyze firms' competitiveness was introduced in Gaddy and Ickes (2002).
2   We address this puzzle directly in Chapter 4.
3   A very robust finding in development economics is that investment rates measured at international prices are correlated with levels and growth rates of output across countries (Hsieh and Klenow 2007 and Restuccia and Urrutia 2001). The concept of international prices is explained in note 16 below.
4   What is the market value of the capital stock? It is that capital stock's contribution to the expected discounted value of future profits. The historical value of the capital stock, in contrast, is the sum of past investment, less depreciation. Given the regime change implied by transition, the probability that the market value would be within an order of magnitude of the historical value, let alone the same, must be very close to zero. Even in market economies the two quantities do not coincide, but on average they would be close. The problem in Russia is the systematic bias: the market value is systematically lower than the historical value, and the difference is at least an order of magnitude.
5   Even those that recognize that much of the capital stock is junk assume that there is enough so that with proper institutions productivity increases would occur. What this view ignores is the write-off issue. Alternatively, it assumes that because capital has no market value it can be freely disposed of (in the economy-wide sense). This ignores the political struggle to give it value.
6   Location is an aspect of this as well.
7   A second reason why one should not automatically assume it is correct to push ahead blindly with "good" institutional reforms is that it might sustain false illusions about the outcome.
8   Gaddy and Ickes (2002: 49, fn 10) write: "Improvements in [technical] efficiency involve movements from inside the production frontier to the boundary of the frontier. However, the gain implied by this may not be sufficient to overcome the fact that the enterprise produces the wrong thing in the wrong place."
9   Our discussion in Chapter 3 on location will make it clear why we choose these examples.
10   Connolly (2011) is an exception.

11   It is to be noted that Palmeda and Lewis focus primarily on industry impediments due to lack of competition rather than macro institutional issues such as corruption, lack of labor mobility, or corporate governance.

12   All the arguments we make here with regard to capital apply equally to the resource sector, and the territories where the resources are located. Just because the resources are in the ground does not mean that their extraction has value once you incorporate the full costs of operating in these regions. Notice that these sites were often originally founded on the basis of prison labor – e.g. Norilsk – so the cost of production was clearly shifted on to others. There is, however, one key difference between resources and manufacturing industries. Technological advance (for instance, using Canadian methods) can lower the cost of resource extraction in cold regions, etc., so it may be profitable in the future (which is another reason for keeping the resource in the ground), whereas the dinosaur plant in Perm will never be profitable and time will only cause an increase in d (distance to market, as defined in *Russia's Virtual Economy*).

13   In almost all of the cross-country literature, y (per-capita GDP) is measured at international prices while i (the investment share of GDP) is measured at domestic prices. See Levine and Renelt (1992), for example. The literature does not seem to take notice of this. We discuss the implications of this below.

14   A country's geographical location and climate, for instance, are among the variables that impact growth, and one could argue that they cannot be changed. However, as we discuss in Chapter 3, a country such as Russia could change the location of its industry and population within its fixed boundaries.

15   The forecasting model used by Sutela is the Levine–Renelt equation with actual values for Russia inserted on the right-hand side. In our notation his equation is:
$$y_j = -0.83 - .35*y_{0,j} - .38*n_j + 3.17*sec_j + 17.5*i_j$$

16   International prices are created by calculating purchasing power parity prices for all goods and services. The Penn World Tables, created by Irving Kravis, Alan Heston, and Robert Summers, created a comparable set of national accounts that could be used to compare countries. The data have appeared in a series of versions, or generations, since 1970, which vary by the year of the price collection done by the International Comparison Project, which collects prices for the same or similar goods in different countries. One problem that has been noticed is that the data are highly variable between versions (see Johnson *et al.* 2009 for discussion and details). We have therefore used the data from version 6.3 exclusively throughout.

17   Like so many other aspects of economic policy, what was merely a disease in developing countries was a pathology in the socialist world.

18   In principle, the concept of high and low is relative to an international benchmark. In practice, the Penn World Tables uses the United States as a benchmark. So if the relative price is greater than unity it means that the cost of increasing capital (in terms of foregone domestic consumption) is higher than in the US.

19   This was first noted by Summers and Heston (1991).

20 This has been intensively analyzed by Richard Ericson (1999). Essentially, costs of investment were shifted, under Soviet pricing rules, onto consumption. This was an implicit tax on consumption to finance investment. When price liberalization occurs investment goods must cover their costs, so their relative price rises.

21 Notice that much of this divergence is caused by Russia and Ukraine.

22 Data for our attainment variable are from Barro and Lee (2010). (In the Barro–Lee education data, appendix A2, it is the sum of "second level, total" and "post-secondary level, total.") Had we estimated our equation using L–R's SEC instead of our BLSEC, the coefficient on investment would rise to 14.6 with a t-statistic of 6.3.

23 See Ofer (1987) for a discussion of the Soviet growth record and extensive growth.

24 It is important to note that the regression results are based on a cross section of countries where investment rates never reached the range that we are considering here. The results presume that the coefficients will be constant in the relevant range, but we are considering an extension far out of that range.

25 See Gaddy and Ickes (2010) and forthcoming for a discussion of rent addiction.

26 We discuss this issue at length in *Russia's Virtual Economy* (Gaddy and Ickes 2002).

27 The transition to a market economy should have been a cataclysmic event for dinosaur enterprises, just as the K-T event at the end of the Cretaceous Period was fatal for the dinosaurs. Dinosaur enterprises, however, were able to survive by using their relational capital to obtain rents. See Ickes (2003).

28 Ironically, support for the dinosaurs often comes from the incomes of the oligarchs. One might be tempted to say that in this case, rather than enriching them, such policies tax them. Of course, however, the oligarchs participate in these policies precisely because this allows them to indeed "enrich themselves" by exploiting the assets that they obtained. See Gaddy and Ickes (2002, 2011).

29 This work builds on that of Ciccone (2002), who emphasized the productivity-enhancing impact of adopting industrial technologies along chains of production. Multiplier effects work in both directions.

30 Note that throughout this discussion we have ignored the issue of quality of capital goods. But inferior-quality goods have a similar effect on production as higher prices.

31 Kravis *et al.* go on to say that the reason investment is counted this way is not because it is the correct approach, but because it is the only feasible one. They explain: "One line of reasoning in response to such questions [as investment to compensate for the cold] is to regard the future flow of services that each capital good would produce in each country as the basis for evaluating the relative amounts of investment. This implies that an international comparison should be made of the present value of the increases in output – ultimately in the form of consumption goods – that new capital goods would contribute in each economy. In the real world, no dated list is available of consumer goods that will eventually flow from new investment, but only the value of investment

in the prices of the capital goods themselves in each country's own currency. Furthermore, knotty problems would arise in isolating the differences in future flow that could be attributed to the input of capital from the differences attributable to other elements, such as other factor inputs and environment. Therefore, it is too difficult to implement the future-flow-of-services approach" (Kravis *et al.* 1982: 29).

32 Casselli (2005: 2) notes: "[T]he consensus view in development accounting is that efficiency plays a very large role. A sentence commonly used to summarize the existing literature sounds something like 'differences in efficiency account for at least 50% of differences in per capita income'."

33 This idea is also consistent with the ideas of Paul Romer. And Mokyr (1990) has referred to technology embodied in machinery as the "lever of riches."

34 That is, if growth caused equipment investment, then we would expect to see the same association with investment in structures. Higher growth would cause demand for both more machinery and more structures to house them. But given that the association is between equipment investment and growth, it is much more likely that the former causes the latter.

35 This is a vital issue which we only reference here. We discuss this issue at much greater length in Chapter 3.

36 One might argue that construction is such a high portion of Russian investment precisely because it is so susceptible to theft. Another important factor, however, is the impact of cold. Construction is more expensive in cold climates. See Chapter 3.

37 This is obviously a bigger problem for investment in the regions than for investment in Moscow, so it could explain why returns are lower in the regions. Some of the extra return attributed to Moscow's location could be due to access to authorities, but the τ-effect implies that this factor may be overstated.

3 The economics of location

1 This should be distinguished from the impact of Russia's resource wealth, which also enabled the planners to pursue economically irrational investments beyond what would have been possible in a less abundant economy. An economy with abundant resources can make wasteful mistakes for much longer before balance of payments difficulties halt the process. That is different from the problem discussed here: the nature of the mistakes that were made.

2 This suggests a fundamental point that we emphasize in this chapter: cold and distance, considered from an economic viewpoint, are not fixed features of Russia's geography, but rather the result of economic decisions.

3 The information and discussion about the economic effects of the cold in the following sections are based on research initiated by the authors in 2000 in a project called the "Cost of the Cold," based at the Brookings Institution's Center for Social and Economic Dynamics (CSED) and Pennsylvania State University Department of Economics. We first reported on this research in Gaddy and Ickes (2001). Some of the output of that project was subsequently published by project members, including in Hill and Gaddy (2003) and Mikhailova (2004).

4   That temperature (which is −90° F) was recorded three times: in Verkhoyansk on February 5 and February 7, 1892, and in Oymyakon on February 6, 1933. Both locations are in the Republic of Sakha (Yakutiya). U.S. National Climatic Data Center, National Oceanic and Atmosphere Administration (NOAA) [http://www.ncdc.noaa.gov/oa/climate/globalextremes.html#lowtemp].

5   In fact, it seems that the real reason the plant was built was that it was part of a gentleman's agreement between US Steel and the State of Minnesota not to impose a significant tax on iron ore in exchange for the construction of an integrated steel plant within the state, whose mines furnished most of the iron ore for US Steel. White and Primmer (1937) is the classic source on this episode, and we draw on it heavily here.

6   This was the name of the wholly owned subsidiary of US Steel that built the works in Duluth.

7   Although Perm is located near large oil deposits, and production began in this region in the early 1930s, production was on a small scale and contributed little to the growth of the metropolitan area. Today Lukoil, Russia's largest private oil company, has significant investments in this area, including refineries. See Alekperov (2011) and Grace (2005) for a discussion of the discovery and exploitation of oil deposits in the Perm region.

8   It is important to note that the gentleman's agreement that led to the initial growth of Duluth was a temporary subvention of economic forces.

9   The best-known example is Andrey Parshev's book, *Why Russia Is Not America* (2000). Parshev argues that, largely because of the cold climate and the costs it imposes on economic activity, Russia is fated to fail as a global competitor and thus should remain outside the world economic community.

10   It should also be noted that, in accounting for the adverse effects of cold on manual tasks, Abele looks exclusively at the physical limitations of cold. He expressly disregards any negative psychological or motivational effects of working in extreme cold.

11   The researchers recognized this, noting that "[a] more exhaustive survey would certainly yield a significantly higher adaptation cost estimate."

12   Of course, the magnitude of private adaptation costs depends on decisions about where to locate. If Canadians are less likely to locate large populations in inhospitable regions – compared with Russia – then they will incur smaller aggregate adaptation costs.

13   It is economically advantageous to locate along the US border as well, as this minimizes the economic distance from trading partners. We discuss this below.

14   Robert Anderson, Jr. (1974) calculated the health costs of cooling. Ralph D'Arge (1974) estimated other economic costs of cooling, including agriculture, forestry, and marine resources. The work on the value of climate amenities drew on the work of Irving Hoch (1977).

15   The DOT work was the basis of the research by Thomas Gale Moore. Moore himself did not use the DOT research to study the costs of the cold but rather the benefits of warmer temperatures. See Moore (1998a, 1998b). Indeed, the data in Table 3.4 are supplemented by Moore's efforts to update some of the costs to account for changes since the 1970s.

16 US GDP in 1990 was about $5,800 billion.

17 This calculation ignores any migration or technological development that makes it possible to cope with a colder climate. It thus assumes that people are forced to suffer the costs of the cold without acting to avoid them. Of course, in Russia TPC fell precisely because people moved to colder climates – a case where migration went the "wrong way."

18 Another important difference between the US and Russia, which we do not consider here, is that in the US case we estimate the cost of an extra degree of cold on an optimally allocated population. Whereas the initial Russian population distribution is far from optimal. Theory would suggest that the cost of change in the Russian case would thus be greater.

19 Note that Table 3.4 relates to "standard Soviet machines" in the 1960s. Technological improvement leads to equipment better suited for the cold. It is costly to develop and produce such improved machines, of course, but it is presumably cheaper than simply pouring in more machines to replace old ones. In the Soviet context, however, the costliness of cold regions was seen as an advantage for vested interests in the heavy equipment manufacturing sector, who saw the regions as a black hole with an seemingly insatiable appetite for more machines.

20 The assumption behind Mikhailova's procedure is not that spatial structures of different market economies should be similar but rather that the dynamic forces that impact on location should be similar. In other words, she does not just compare the existing spatial allocations in Russia and Canada but instead looks at the changes in structure over time: initial conditions matter.

21 Mikhailova tests for the effect of World War II on location policy. "The impact of World War II, however drastic in the case of Russia, explains the east–west misbalance only partly. Even according to the most liberal estimates, the excess population of Siberia and the Far East remains at the level above 9.6 million after the war adjustment, and is statistically significant."

22 We discuss this in the appendix to this chapter.

23 Owing to economies of scale it is not a solution for closed economies either, as the economies of agglomeration lead to clustering even in closed economies.

24 In fact, it turns out that when calculated in this manner the DPC tends to converge rather quickly, so the choice of the 50 largest cities produces a robust result.

25 Note that even without the adjustment for the relative size of the two countries, the US has a larger DPC than Russia: around 2,000 km compared to Russia's 1,700 km. So even in absolute terms, Americans are farther apart than Russians.

26 Even now, there is a repeated call to repopulate Siberia to prevent it from falling to Chinese rule, as if squatting were nine-tenths of the law.

27 US highway data from the US Bureau of Transportation Statistics, "National Transportation Statistics, 2010," available at http://www.bts.gov. In fact, Russia's total of highways with four or more lanes is barely half of the level of that in the state of North Carolina. NC data from North Carolina Department of Transportation, "2010 Highway and Road Mileage Report," p. 13, http://www.ncdot.gov/travel/statemapping/.

28　We cannot escape thinking of the analogy of investing in a first-class video system to play Betamax tapes.

29　Another, more recent, example: on May 5, 2012, the Ministry of Economic Development of Russia proposed a controversial law project "On development of Siberia and the Far East," which contained a proposition to create a "government corporation" to manage and develop these regions of Russia.

30　Goskomstat.

31　Russian internal migration fell by approximately one-half from the Soviet period of the 1980s to the Russian era of the 1990s. See Andrienko and Guriev (2004).

32　The argument that Russia needs to keep Siberia populated to prevent it falling into Chinese hands makes no economic sense. Russia's possession of Siberia relies on its political and military power, not the number of inhabitants in Siberia. Moreover, it is the subsidies to the population in Siberia that attract Chinese immigrants. But the argument seems to have an attraction to the Russian soul.

33　One might be tempted to argue that with a sufficiently large fall in wages in Perm, its relative cost disadvantage could be offset. Yet, we know that even in a market economy that suffered the Great Depression wages did not fall sufficiently to save Duluth's steel industry. Moreover, it typically takes a compensating differential to offset the cold climate. If wages fell, the best workers leave and only those with the poorest prospects remain. Would an entrepreneur choosing between locations choose Perm based on the cheap labor of those who would not leave? Would those workers be enough of a bonus to offset the climate and location handicaps of Perm?

4　Market-impeding federalism

1　Reader comment by a resident of the Russian Far East in *Komsomolskaya pravda*, May 29, 2010.

2　According to the most definitive study on migration in Russia, Andrienko and Guriev (2005), "Throughout more than a decade of economic transition, internal migration rates have been low, and there has been virtually no convergence across regions."

3　Qian and Weingast (1997).

4　At least for the decade of the 1990s, for which we have data.

5　This is not to say that labor mobility is non-existent in Russia. At the level of individual firms labor has been getting increasingly more mobile during the transition period. However, most of labor movement is intersectoral but not interregional. The level of labor migration across regions is still low.

6　Note that capital stock is measured as the base (purchase) value of capital adjusted for depreciation at the official rate, and does not truly represent capital stock used for production. If a region is economically successful and the investment level is high, all new capital correctly shows up in data. If a region is in recession capital is underutilized, and the measured capital stock is actually higher than the utilized capital stock. Probably, capital is even more mobile across regions than it appears to be.

7   Mikhailova (2004: 52–3).

8   In Appendix F of *Russia's Virtual Economy* (Gaddy and Ickes 2002) we developed a model of governor decision-making and collusion with regional interests.

9   In Gaddy and Ickes (2002) we classify such transfers as investments in relational capital on the part of the firms.

10 Blanchard–Shleifer use a for this parameter. Otherwise our notation is the same as theirs.

11 In practice this could include tax sharing, tax assignments, and transfers. The key point is that α represents what the region ends up with from increased growth regardless of how the sharing takes place.

12 Appointing governors by no means guarantees that they will follow all the orders of the central government. Even Stalin could not prevent officials from being captured by local interests.

13 This is thus a Brezhnevite system of incentives rather than a Stalinist incentive system.

14 This assumption is a result of their interest in comparing China with Russia. This assumption is problematic, and we will drop it shortly. Most of our concern in this chapter is with the heterogeneity of regions within Russia.

15 Notice that Blanchard and Shleifer do not subject b to any resource constraint, although, obviously, there is a limit to how much looting there can be. We follow their interpretation in the subsequent analysis.

16 What they ignore is an important structural difference. In China industry is not geographically specialized; in Russia it is. So, for insurance reasons alone, the optimal contract would have more fiscal federalism in Russia, hence lower α. For an empirical analysis of how fiscal transfers are related to structural differences in Russia, see Narayan 1999. Hence we focus below on differences across regions.

17 For example, Zhuravskaya (2000) finds marginal α to be as low as 0.1 between the bottom two layers of government.

18 Blanchard and Shleifer (2001: 178) write: "As best we can tell, the economic benefits of decentralization obtained from federalism rely crucially on some form of political centralization. Without such centralization, the incentives to pursue regionalist policies are too high, and cannot be eliminated solely through clever economic and fiscal arrangements." Of course, the period of Putin's rule has seen a steady increase in central authority with very little change in the amount of reform. Perhaps there are other factors at work.

19 It is always important to distinguish growth and welfare. Markets improve efficiency and welfare, but sometimes the efficient thing to do is shrink.

20 Unless they can be provided by a central government that redistributes across regions. But this requires a strong center, which is their main point.

21 We repeat our earlier point that these are still Brezhnevite as opposed to Stalinist incentives, which involved the Gulag and worse. In the present system the governor can always walk away – all he loses is his bonus.

22 A crucial question remains over why local governments are more likely to be anti-growth than the central government. Blanchard and Shleifer explain this by arguing that larger units are less likely to be captured and that big oligarchs may be less anti-growth than local ones. This may sometimes be the case, but it is hard to see why it is a general principle. A better explanation for why some regional officials are anti-growth is that they preside over loser regions. If they have a large share of dinosaurs, then policies that will be conducive to growth may also be conducive to growth elsewhere. The key point is that restructuring in Russia has a serious regional aspect to it and the governors realize this, so they act accordingly. In this regard the comments of Viktor Tolokonskiy, governor of Novosibirsk oblast (August 2000), are instructive: "Under conditions of total openness of the economy ... we here in Siberia should not expect any serious investment activity at all. Our costs of production are too high, residential housing and office manufacturing facilities are too expensive, and our transport costs and wages are higher than in southeastern Asia."

23 It is not just that regional boundaries in Russia are not the endogenous result of efficient economic location at some time in the past. Boundaries in Russia have always been the result of administrative control efforts designed to extract rents. But during the Soviet period the lack of market pricing led to further misperceptions of value creation and to a distribution of population and economic activity fully divorced from any market rationality. This is the environment on which federalism is imposed in Russia.

24 Lant Pritchett (2006) introduced the notion of "geographic zombie countries," which captures a similar intuition on the international dimension. These are "countries whose current labor force far exceeds the quantity of labor demanded consistent with high (or adequate) wages even at the best imaginable policies and institutions." The reduction of labor demand in such countries is typically the result of "large, persistent, negative, geographic-specific productivity shocks." Normally, they begin to become "ghost countries," as population migrates out. "However," he continues, "if outward labor mobility is limited, this will lead the adjustment to come not in changes in population but in wages, so countries will be 'zombies' – the 'living ghosts' – with falling wages and incomes."

25 What would it mean for $p \rightarrow \infty$? This means that with 100 percent certainty the governor is fired for not pursuing reform. But even this does not cause reform because no stick is sufficient when $y < 0$. A new kind of carrot (one that comes from outside the region) is needed.

26 Although we do not analyze this, one could argue that foreign aid or a budget deficit is required to maintain high incentives for winner regions. This allows the budget balance condition to be broken. In our analysis, however, α is fixed.

27 In this formulation the additional transfer payment covers the loss, and the governor's payoff from pro-reform is then p multiplied by the sum $\alpha y_j + \phi$. Our assumption is thus that the governor receives the payoff only if he stays in power, hence the payoff appears inside the brackets in (4.2).

28 Introducing ϕ is a simple way to make the net transfer to a region dependent on its growth possibilities.

29   In the general case this constraint would be $\sum_{j \in J} \phi_j \leq \sum_{i \in I} (1 - \alpha_i) y_i$ where J and I are the sets of loser and winner regions, respectively.

30   Indeed, we are quite certain that this is the case in Russia.

31   Of course, there are also benefits to certain owners of assets. We assume for now that the cost of congestion outweighs the gain to rentiers. Otherwise, it would be hard to understand why rich countries limit migration. The potential gains from international migration dwarf all other known policies to help the poor. See, for example, Klein and Ventura (2009). Labor productivity in the US and other leading industrialized countries is so much higher than in India that world income would rise dramatically with a large reallocation of labor to high productivity countries. However, citizens of rich countries do not appear to be sufficiently persuaded of these benefits to open their borders.

32   It could also be argued, for example, that the benefits take longer to accrue than the costs. This may be especially true in Russia, where any capital flow to the winner regions is likely to be very gradual if it occurs at all.

33   Notice that η_i is the congestion cost to the winner region of in-migration from other regions due to reform in region i. This differs from the congestion cost imposed on region i from reform in region j, which we denote as η_{ij}.

34   Recall the quote that opens this chapter.

35   For simplicity we are assuming that the payment needed to keep the lights on is sufficient to prevent out-migration. Basically, if the side payment is made then out-migration is completely eliminated

36   To prevent confusion we use the term "subsidies" to refer to the payments made to keep the lights on and "side payments" to refer to the transfers made to induce reform in loser regions. These choices are not intended to provide any moral characterization, nor are they based on a rigorous distinction.

37   If j does not reform it does not receive the side payment, which means that i does not pay the additional tax.

38   We are focusing here on the choice for region i given that it is choosing to reform, so we can ignore η_i as it appears on both sides of equation (4.6), and focus on the consequences of the decision in region j, that is on η_{ij}.

39   Following Blanchard and Shleifer, the model is static. A dynamic model would compare the expected present value of the costs and benefits of reform over the official's horizon.

40   There is an extra effect from "lights on" that we have not analyzed. By encouraging Perm not to reform, Moscow not only saves congestion costs but also becomes relatively more attractive for foreign direct investment (FDI). This happens at the cost of losing some domestic investment that could come from Perm. But it may well be that Moscow values the FDI much more highly. And in fact the concentration of FDI in Moscow has been increasing in recent times.

41   Moscow's economic success is not predicated on cheap labor. It has utilized migrant labor for construction, but continues to limit in-migration of a permanent population. Moscow's economic success has more to do with being

the financial and economic capital of the country and headquarters of the companies that dominate the resource sectors.

42   Each unit in the chain must bargain with a supplier and a customer. There is Nash bargaining at each step, so that the surplus is split, given the symmetry of the situation. The value of the surplus in the last stage (bargaining between the final producer and the last intermediate producer) is 1. This follows because the value of the good at stage n is still zero. So the last intermediate producer gets one-half of the surplus, 1/2. Now what happens at the prior stage? The surplus here is 1/2, so the next-to-last intermediate producer and the last producer each get 1/4. Continue in this fashion and it follows that the first intermediate producer gets $\left(\frac{1}{2}\right)^n$. The surplus available to split at the first stage is $\left(\frac{1}{2}\right)^n - c$, since the first producer must purchase the primary input to produce. Clearly then we must have $c < \left(\frac{1}{2}\right)^n$ in order for there to be positive surplus to split. If $c > \left(\frac{1}{2}\right)^n$, then the primary producer will prefer to sell to someone else. Notice that c does not need to be all that large to trigger defection. Suppose the primary producer defects. The magnitude of the fall in output? It could be as large as $1 - \left(\frac{1}{2}\right)^n$. Thus rather meager private opportunities can cause a rather large fall in output. Blanchard and Kremer interpret n as the level of complexity of production. As n increases, the likelihood of defection increases exponentially.

43   Notice that in this case with $c > 1$ it is not bargaining that is the problem. Rather it is the value destruction that takes place along the chain of production.

44   Indeed, it could be argued that presiding over a declining region is even worse for an appointed governor. At least the elected governor is losing unhappy voters.

45   And even today "lights on" is supplemented in Moscow by the requirement of *propiska*.

46   See Ericson (2002) for an analysis of Russia's industrial feudalism.

47   There is an important contrast between real capital and fictitious capital. The former requires a compensating differential to locate in the east. Existing capital may be sunk, but new investment would follow labor to warmer regions. Indeed, if labor migrated and the capital–labor ratio led to a rise in the real wage, this would make it more difficult to earn rents in the east, further inhibiting new investment in the east. But fictitious capital is sunk.

48   The reason is that subsidies can be attracted only if there is labor – population – in the regions.

5 Human capital

1   The most comprehensive summary of Russia's current condition with respect to all these human capital components is Eberstadt (2010). Our descriptive statistics in the following are based on many of the same and similar sources as used by Eberstadt. Our interpretations of the causes and consequences of the phenomena and trends sometimes differ from his, however.

2   Unless otherwise indicated, all historical Russian population statistics are from the Russian State Committee on Statistics (GKS).

3   Russia ranked 151 out of 159 countries in population growth rate between 1990 and 2008 according to Angus Maddison's dataset "Historical Statistics of the World Economy: 1–2008 AD." See "Table 4: Population Growth Rates, 1950–2030," at http://www.ggdc.net/MADDISON/oriindex.htm, which is included within the "Historical Statistics" and can be found by clicking on the link "Statistics on World Population, GDP and Per Capita GDP, 1–2008 AD".

4   That there is some connection between the population decline and the communist past seems hard to dispute. Of the 17 countries of the world that lost any population at all in the 1990–2008 period, 16 were former communist countries of Eastern and Central Europe. (The sole exception was Trinidad and Tobago, which lost around 25,000 residents.) Not all the successor states of the USSR lost population: the Muslim countries of Central Asia grew. But here, too, the communist legacy seems important, since even though they are growing, Muslim former Soviet countries have population growth rates that are considerably lower than Muslim countries without a communist past. The "communism penalty" to population dynamics is roughly the same for Muslim and non-Muslim countries: population growth in the typical former communist country was about 0.8–1.0 percentage points lower per year in the 1995–2009 period compared to the peer group of countries (non-Muslim and Muslim) without a communist past. Compared to the other non-Muslim republics of the former USSR, Russia did not fare so poorly. Combined, those other non-Muslim former Soviet republics (Armenia, Belarus, Estonia, Georgia, Latvia, Lithuania, Moldova, and Ukraine) had population loss rates that were on average twice as high as Russia's. The world leader in population loss in 1990–2008 was NATO and EU member Bulgaria, which shrank more than four times as fast as Russia. [All data from http://www.ggdc.net/MADDISON/oriindex.htm "Historical Statistics of the World Economy: 1–2008 AD."]

5   There may be, of course, a Great Power consideration of population size for military needs, but this is clearly not an economic welfare consideration. It is presumably easier, however, to complain about lack of population growth as an economic impediment.

6   The importance of the dependency ratio for growth prospects of developing countries has been studied by Bloom and Williamson (1997) and Bloom *et al.* (2001), who emphasized the role of the demographic dividend in explaining the performance of the Asian Tigers.

7   Since working age differs from country to country, the definitions of "young" and "old" necessarily also differ. We define the working age segment of the population as all men and women between the ages of 20 and 64.

8   See Denisova (2009) for a recent independent analysis and discussion of other studies, Russian and Western.

9   Exactly what is causing the heavy drinking itself, however, is not clear. Some scholars have pointed to the relative cheapening of alcohol, particularly vodka, as the key determinant of rising alcohol consumption. See, e.g., Treisman (2010). There is no question that vodka has become more affordable in Russia, as the relative price of vodka has declined and incomes have risen. In the second half of

the 1990s the average worker could buy about 25 liters of vodka for his monthly wage. By 2004 he could buy 50 liters. In 2011 the wage was equal to the price of 92.5 liters of vodka (authors' calculations based on wage and price data from Goskomstat). On the other hand, despite the growing affordability of vodka, official sales per capita have not risen in the past few years. In her micro-analysis Denisova (2009) found that the relative price of alcohol was a statistically insignificant factor in mortality.

10   The most likely scenario is an initial decline in the dependency ratio simply because the working age cohort is larger. But this effect is likely to be temporary, as members of the working age cohort age and survive longer, the dependency ratio will rise. Depending on the rate of population growth it could even rise higher than the initial level.

11   We discuss health (or lack of health) separately from mortality, even though morbidity (prevalence of disease) is of course closely connected to and correlated with mortality. Indeed, empirical work on health frequently uses measures of mortality – life expectancies, survival rates, death rates – as proxies for health because the data are more readily accessible. Strictly speaking, however, morbidity and mortality may have different economic impacts, and thus different implications for economic growth. The death of an individual will reduce the actual or potential stock of human capital (if the person is of working age or younger). If that person were instead to fall victim to a permanently debilitating illness, but survive, there would be the same loss of human capital but in addition there would be an extra burden as the person also now joins the ranks of the non-productive. In that sense morbidity can be worse than mortality. This could be another example of the τ-effect. Suppose that Russia has significantly higher morbidity than other countries. Since Russia has high educational attainment, it accumulates significant human capital. (This assumes that the quality of the education is high – a point we examine later). But if morbidity is high, much of this human capital cannot be used. So measured human capital is higher than actual, effective, human capital.

12   Another way to think of these results is to say that Russia has already reaped the reward from health improvements. It had its "developing country health boom" in the 1920s and 1930s, as a result of early Bolshevik policies of centralized health care. The central planning system was good at large-scale interventions to manage health risks at the *public* level (for instance, controlling infectious diseases). It was bad at promoting the kinds of lifestyle changes on the *private* level that reduce the risks of heart disease, certain cancers, and the like.

13   In terms of Figure 5.15 an improvement in Russia's ASR would result in a vertical shift to the trend line rather than to the northeast.

14   Data from OECD's *Education at a Glance 2011: OECD Indicators*. Table A1.2a, "Population with at least upper secondary education (2009)," and Table A1.3a, "Population with tertiary education (2009)," http://www.oecd.org/education/skills-beyond-school/48630299.pdf. Note that while the OECD countries are reporting 2009 data, Russia's data are from 2002.

15   PISA measures the performance of 15-year-olds: that is, students in the mid-level of secondary school. Some 70 countries have taken part in PISA since it began in 2000, accounting for more than 90 percent of the world economy.

Around 470,000 students participated in PISA 2009, representing about 26 million 15-year-olds. *PISA 2009 Results: What Students Know and Can Do: Student Performance in Reading, Mathematics and Science* (Volume I), OECD 2010.

16 Beyond the low scores in themselves, the conclusions of a World Bank study on why Russians do not score higher on the PISA tests are extra cause for concern. The reason Russian students lag behind their counterparts in other countries, the authors write, is that the ability "to reproduce knowledge and apply known algorithms dominates in the profile of achievements of Russian students in comparison with the high-level intellectual skills (generalization, analysis, forecasting, generation of hypotheses, and so forth)." Nikolaev and Chugunov 2012: 34–5.

17 Information about the Shanghai rankings is available at http://www.shanghairank-ing.com/index.html; the *Times* rankings at http://www.timeshighereducation.co.uk/world-university-rankings and the QS rankings at http://www.topuniversi-ties.com/. The methodologies of the rankings differ somewhat. The Shanghai rankings place great emphasis on research results and "superstar" status of faculty and alumni (number of Nobel Prize and other award winners, etc.). The other two are based mainly on peer surveys and give weight also to teaching.

18 We should point out that producing brilliant innovators such as Sergey Brin, serves no purpose for Russia's growth unless they stay inside Russia and do not permanently emigrate to the United States (as did Google co-founder Brin).

19 One might object that the same holds true for physical capital, that is, "two railcars cannot substitute for an oil well." But the difference is, one can sell a railcar and buy an oil well. This cannot be done with the humanities PhDs.

20 See Gaddy and Ickes (forthcoming).

21 Of course, like the rest of the profession, we use a production function that ignores energy as a primary factor, and therefore understate the impact of resource wealth in explaining Russian performance. The impact of resource wealth is showing up in TFP.

22 The case of Sverdlovsk oblast is a good example. Between 2004 and 2005 its urban share allegedly dropped from 88 percent to 83 percent, a fact which, if true, would have involved a sudden mass migration of city dwellers to the countryside. What actually happened was that the regional statistics agency reclassified some 70 "population points" as rural rather than urban. No real population shift took place.

6 Conclusion

1 There is another hypothetical alternative: Comprehensive reform implemented by an autocrat who can shut down the dinosaurs and nationalize resource indus-tries and use the rents to compensate the losers, who will be many. Nationalization of resource producers would be necessary to be able to buy off all the losers from a shutdown of the dinosaurs. This comprehensive reform would thus be impossible without Stalinist repression. It may have been possible to do this in

a non-autocratic way at the start of reform in 1992, but that road was not taken. Now an autocrat would certainly be needed, but it is hard to believe that even this would be sufficient today. Stalinist repression would make it impossible to engage the investments necessary to keep Russian rents flowing. Moreover, there is no sign that Putin has the stomach, or the inclination, for this.

2   We use Skolkovo as emblematic of efforts to diversify the Russian economy away from resources by emphasizing innovation and technology. Skolkovo would be an appropriate straw man if it were not actually an active element of government policy.

3   In part, the Protection Racket represents a mechanism to enforce tax compliance on the part of the resource companies. Even more importantly, it ensures that the companies pay a sort of informal tax by placing production orders with the heavy manufacturers, something we describe as "rent-sharing through production."

4   We first discussed the notion of political impermissibility in the Russian context in Gaddy and Ickes (2002).

5   Putin's rhetoric in announcing the defense modernization program was notable: "We will have to modernize the entire defense industry and the way it works, and carry out the same kind of comprehensive and powerful modernization drive that was achieved in the 1930s." Transcript of Putin's remarks at the "expanded-format Security Council meeting" on August 31, 2012, at http://eng.kremlin.ru/transcripts/4343.

6   Initially, Putin presented his defense modernization effort as an economic driver. See, for example, his statement in an October 7, 2001, speech that "investments of ... substantial resources in the defense industry will contribute to the modernization of the entire Russian economy." After the street protests in December 2011 he placed more emphasis on its social role in preserving jobs and supporting industrial cities. The theme of "defense industry versus Moscow" was prominent in Putin's nationally televised dialogue with the nation on December 15, 2011, when he repeatedly invoked the contrast between defense industry workers and the Moscow protesters. During that broadcast, a group of workers from the famous Uralvagonzavod tank plant in the city of Nizhnyy Tagil (Sverdlovsk oblast) even offered to come to Moscow to help quell the protests. One of Putin's first acts after assuming the presidency was to appoint the very worker who had made the offer, a certain Igor Kholmanskikh, to the important position of presidential plenipotentiary for the entire Urals region.

7   It is crucial to note just how significant is Russia's comparative advantage in resources. As we noted in Gaddy and Ickes (2010: 290): "let us suppose that Russia had undertaken a diversification program in 2000. What is the likelihood that this would have resulted in success by the summer of 2008? Over that period, 2000–2008, the increase in annual export earnings from commodities was more than 20 times greater than the increased yearly income from manufacturing exports. The magnitude of investment that would have been required to even come close to balancing those shares is mind-boggling."

8   The classic reference is Wright and Czelusta (2006).

References

Abele, Gunars, 1986. "Effect of Cold Weather on Productivity," *in Technology Transfer Opportunities for the Construction Engineering Community, Proceedings of Construction Seminar, Denver, CO*, February 1986, U.S. Army Cold Regions Research and Engineering Laboratory, pp. 61–6.

Acemoglu, Daron, and Simon Johnson, 2007. "Disease and Development: The Effect of Life Expectancy on Economic Growth," *Journal of Political Economy* 115 (6), pp. 925–85.

Akerlof, George, Andrew Rose, Janet Yellen, and Helga Hesenius, 1991. "East Germany in from the Cold: The Economic Aftermath of Currency Union," *Brookings Papers on Economic Activity* 1, pp. 1–105.

Alekperov, Vagit, 2011. *Oil of Russia. Past, Present, and Future*. East View Press.

Anderson, Robert Jr., 1974. "The Health Costs of Changing Macro-Climates," in *Proceedings of the Third Conference on the Climatic Impact Assessment Program*, ed. Anthony Broderick and Thomas M. Hard, DOT-TSC-OST-74-15, pp. 582–92.

Andrienko, Yuri, and Sergei Guriev, 2004. "Determinants of Interregional Mobility in Russia: Evidence from Panel Data," *Economics of Transition* 12 (1), pp. 1–27.

Andrienko, Yuri, and Sergei Guriev, 2005. "Understanding Migration in Russia," NES/CEFIR Working Paper, 23.

Ashraf, Quamrul H., Ashley Lester, and David N. Weil, 2008. "When Does Improving Health Raise GDP?" NBER Working Paper 14449.

Barro, Robert and Jong-Wha Lee, 2010. "A New Data Set of Educational Attainment in the World, 1950–2010," NBER Working Paper 15902.

Bhargava, Alok, Dean Jamison, Lawrence J. Lau, and Christopher Murray, 2001. "Modeling the Effects of Health on Economic Growth," *Journal of Health Economics* 20 (3), pp. 423–40.

Blanchard, Olivier and Michael Kremer, 1997. "Disorganization," *The Quarterly Journal of Economics* 112 (4), pp. 1091–126.

Blanchard, Olivier, and Andrei Shleifer, 2001. "Federalism With and Without Political Centralization. China versus Russia," IMF Staff Papers, Volume 48, Special Issue.

Bloom, David, and Jeffrey Williamson, 1997. "Demographic Transitions and Economic Miracles in Emerging Asia," NBER Working Paper 6268.

Bloom, David, David Canning, and Jaypee Sevilla, 2001. "Economic Growth and the Demographic Transition," NBER Working Paper 8685.

Casselli, Francesco, 2005. "Accounting for Cross-Country Income Differences," in *Handbook of Economic Growth, Volume 1A*, ed. Philippe Aghion and Steven N. Durlauf. Amsterdam; London, Elsevier B.V., pp. 679–741.

Ciccone, Antonio, 2002. "Input Chains and Industrialization," *The Review of Economic Studies* 69 (3), pp. 565–87.

Connolly, Richard, 2011. "Financial Constraints on the Modernization of the Russian Economy," *Eurasian Geography and Economics* 52 (3), pp. 428–59.

Crafts, Nicholas, and Kai Kaiser, 2004. "Long Term Growth Prospects in Transition Economies: A Reappraisal," *Structural Change and Economic Dynamics* 15 (1), pp. 101–18.

D'Arge, Ralph, 1974. "Economic Impact of Climate Change: Introduction and Overview," in *Proceedings of the Third Conference on the Climatic Impact Assessment Program*, ed. Anthony Broderick and Thomas M. Hard, DOT-TSC-OST-74-15, pp. 582–92.

De Long, J. Bradford, and Lawrence H. Summers, 1991. "Equipment Investment and Economic Growth," *Quarterly Journal of Economics* 106 (2), pp. 445–502.

De Long, J. Bradford, and Lawrence H. Summers, 1993. "How Strongly do Developing Economies Benefit from Equipment Investment?" *Journal of Monetary Economics* 32 (3), pp. 395–416.

Denisova, Irina, 2009. "Mortality in Russia: Microanalysis," Centre for Economic and Financial Research at New Economic School Working Paper No. 128.

Dogayev, Yu. M., 1969. *Ekonomicheskaya effektivnost' novoy tekhniki na Severe.* Moscow, Nauka.

Domar, Evsey, 1970. "The Causes of Slavery and Serfdom: A Hypothesis," *Journal of Economic History* 30 (1), pp. 18–32.

Eberstadt, Nicholas, 2010. *Russia's Peacetime Demographic Crisis: Dimensions, Causes, Implications.* National Bureau of Asian Research.

Ericson, Richard E., 2002. "The Russian Economy: Market in Form but Feudal in Content," in *Institutional Change in Transition Economies*, ed. Michael Cuddy and Ruvin Gekker. Aldershot, Ashgate, pp. 3–34.

Ericson, Richard, 1999. "The Structural Barrier to Transition Hidden in Input–Output Tables of Centrally Planned Economies," *Economic Systems*, 23 (3), pp. 199–224.

Fischer, Stanley, and Ratna Sahay, 2000. "The Transition After Ten Years," IMF Working Paper, WP/00/30.

Gaddy, Clifford G., 1996. *The Price of the Past.* Washington DC, Brookings Institution Press.

Gaddy, Clifford G., and Barry W. Ickes, 2001. "The Cost of the Cold," Working Paper, Pennsylvania State University.

Gaddy, Clifford G., and Barry W. Ickes, 2002. *Russia's Virtual Economy.* Washington DC, Brookings Institution Press.

Gaddy, Clifford G., and Barry W. Ickes, 2009. "Putin's Third Way," *The National Interest.* http://nationalinterest.org/article/putins-third-way-2958.

Gaddy, Clifford G., and Barry W. Ickes, 2010. "Russia after the Global Financial Crisis," *Eurasian Geography and Economics* 51 (3), pp. 281–311.

Gaddy, Clifford G., and Barry W. Ickes, 2011. "Putin's Protection Racket," in *From Soviet Plans to Russian Reality: Essays in Honor of Pekka Sutela*, ed. Iikka Korhonen and Laura Solanko. Helsinki, WSOYpro Oy.

Gaddy, Clifford G., and Barry W. Ickes, 2013. "Russia's Dependence on Resources," in *The Oxford Handbook of the Russian Economy*, ed. Michael V. Alexeev and Shlomo Weber. Oxford, Oxford University Press.

Gaddy, Clifford G., and Barry W. Ickes, forthcoming. *Russia's Addiction: The Political Economy of Resource Dependence*. Washington DC, Brookings Press.

Grace, John D., 2005. *Russian Oil Supply: Performance and Prospects*. Oxford, Oxford University Press.

Griffiths, John F., 1996. "Some Problems of Regionality in Applications of Climate Change," in *Proceedings of the Fourteenth International Congress of Biometeorology*, September 1–8 1996. Ljubljana, Slovenia, pp. 384–90.

Hall, Robert, 1991. *Booms and Recessions in a Noisy Economy*. New Haven, CT, Yale University Press.

Hanushek, E.A., and L. Wößmann, 2010. "Education and Economic Growth," in *International Encyclopedia of Education*, ed. Penelope Peterson, Eva Baker, and Barry McGaw. Oxford: Elsevier, vol. 2, pp. 245–52.

Herbert, Deborah, and Ian Burton, 1994. "Estimated Costs of Adaptation to Canada's Current Climate and Trends Under Climate Change," unpublished paper. Toronto, Atmospheric Environment Service.

Hill, Fiona, and Clifford Gaddy, 2003. *The Siberian Curse: How Communist Planners Left Russia Out in the Cold*. Washington DC, Brookings Institution Press.

Hoch, Irving, 1977. "Variations in the Quality of Urban Life Among Cities and Regions," in *Public Economics and the Quality of Life*, ed. Lowdon Wingo and Alan Evans. Baltimore, MD, Johns Hopkins Press.

Hsieh, Chang-Tai, and Peter J. Klenow, 2007. "Relative Prices and Relative Prosperity," *American Economic Review* 97 (3), pp. 562–85.

Ickes, Barry W., 2003. "Evolution and Transition," in *Political Economy of Transition and Development*, ed. N. Campos and J. Fidrmuc. Boston, Kluwer.

Ickes, Barry W., and Gur Ofer, 2006. "The Political Economy of Structural Change in Russia," *European Journal of Political Economy* 22 (2), pp. 409–34.

Johnson, Simon, William Larson, Chris Papageorgiou, and Arvind Subramanian, 2009. "Is Newer Better? Penn World Table Revisions and Their Impact on Growth Estimates," NBER Working Paper 15455.

Jones, Charles I., 2011. "Intermediate Goods and Weak Links in the Theory of Economic Development," *American Economic Journal: Macroeconomics* 3, pp. 1–28.

Jorgenson, Dale W., 1990. "Productivity and Economic Growth," in *Fifty Years of Economic Measurement: The Jubilee of the Conference on Research in Income and Wealth*, ed. Ernst R. Berndt and Jack E. Triplett. Chicago, IL, University of Chicago Press, pp. 19–118.

Klein, Paul, and Gustavo Ventura, 2004. "TFP Differences and the Effects of Factor Mobility," Working Paper, Penn State University.

Klein, Paul, and Gustavo Ventura, 2009. "Productivity Differences and the Dynamic Effects of Labor Movements," *Journal of Monetary Economics* 56 (8), pp. 1059–73.

Kravis, Irving B., Alan Heston, and Robert Summers, 1982. *World Product and Income: International Comparisons of Real Gross Product*. Baltimore, MD, Johns Hopkins University Press.

Levine, Ross, and D. Renelt, 1992. "A Sensitivity Analysis of Cross-Country Growth Regressions," *American Economic Review* 82, pp. 942–63.

Lopez-Casanovas, Guillem, Berta Rivera, and Luis Currais, 2005. *Health and Economic Growth: Findings and Policy Implications*. Cambridge, MA, MIT Press.

Mikhailova, Tatiana, 2004. "Essays on Russian Economic Geography: Measuring Spatial Inefficiency," PhD dissertation, The Pennsylvania State University.

Mokyr, Joel, 1990. *The Lever of Riches*, New York, Oxford University Press.

Moore, Thomas Gale, 1998a. *Climate of Fear: Why We Shouldn't Worry about Global Warming*, Washington DC, Cato Institute.

Moore, Thomas Gale, 1998b. "Health and Amenity Effects of Global Warming," *Economic Inquiry* 36, pp. 471–88.

Mote, Victor L., 1983. "Environmental Constraints to the Economic Development of Siberia," in *Soviet Natural Resources in the World Economy*, ed. Robert G. Jensen, T. Shabad, and A. Wright. Chicago, University of Chicago Press, p. 22.

Narayan, R. Badri, 1999. "An Examination of Intergovernmental Transfers in the Russian Federation," PhD dissertation, The Pennsylvania State University.

Nikolaev, Denis, and Dmitry Chugunov, 2012. *The Education System in the Russian Federation: Education Brief 2012*, World Bank.

OECD, 2010. *PISA 2009 Results: What Students Know and Can Do: Student Performance in Reading, Mathematics and Science*, vol. I, OECD.

OECD, 2011. *Education at a Glance 2011: OECD Indicators*. http://www.oecd-ilibrary.org/education/education-at-a-glance-2011_eag_highlights-2011-en.

Ofer, Gur, 1987. "Soviet Economic Growth: 1928–1985," *Journal of Economic Literature* 25 (4), pp. 1767–833.

Palmeda, Vincent, and Bill Lewis, 2001. "Unlocking Economic Growth in Russia," in *Russia's Economic Future: A Compendium of Papers, Joint Economic Committee*, US Congress, pp. 47–80.

Parshev, Andrey, 2000. *Pochemu Rossiya ne Amerika: Kniga dlya tekh, kto ostayetsya zdes'*. Moscow: Krymskiy Most-9D, Forum.

Pritchett, Lant, 2006. "Boom Towns and Ghost Countries: Geography, Agglomeration, and Population Mobility," in *Brookings Trade Forum 2006: Global Labor Markets?*, ed. Susan M. Collins and Carol Graham. Washington DC, Brookings Institution Press, pp. 1–56.

Qian, Yingyi, and Barry R. Weingast, 1997. "Federalism as a Commitment to Preserving Market Incentives," *Journal of Economic Perspectives* 11 (4), pp. 83–92.

Restuccia, D., and C. Urrutia, 2001. "Relative Prices and Investment Rates," *Journal of Monetary Economics* 47, pp. 93–121

Schmitz, J., 2001. "Government Production of Investment Goods and Aggregate Labor Productivity," *Journal of Monetary Economics* 47, pp. 163–87.

Smith, Adam, 1937. *An Inquiry into the Nature and Causes of the Wealth of Nations*, New York, Modern Library.

Summers, Robert, and Alan Heston, 1991. "The Penn World Tables (Mark 5): An Expanded Set of International Comparisons, 1950–88," *Quarterly Journal of Economics* 106 (2), pp. 327–68.

Sutela, Pekka, 2003. *The Russian Market Economy*, Helsinki, Kikimora.

Treisman, Daniel, 2010. "Death and Prices. The Political Economy of Russia's Alcohol Crisis," *Economics of Transition* 18 (2), pp. 281–331.

Weil, David N., 2007. "Accounting for the Effect of Health on Economic Growth," *Quarterly Journal of Economics* 122 (3), pp. 1265–306.

Weingast, Barry R., 1995. "The Economic Role of Political Institutions: Market-Preserving Federalism and Economic Growth," *Journal of Law, Economics and Organization* 11, pp. 1–31.

White, Langdon, and George Primmer, 1937. "The Iron and Steel Industry of Duluth: A Study in Locational Maladjustment," *Geographical Review* 27 (1), pp. 82–91.

Wright, Gavin, and Jesse Czelusta, 2006. "Resource-Based Growth Past and Present," in *Neither Curse nor Destiny: Natural Resources and Development*, ed. Daniel Lederman and William Maloney. Stanford University Press and World Bank Publication.

Zhuravskaya, E., 2000. "Incentives to Provide Local Public Goods: Fiscal Federalism, Russian Style," *Journal of Public Economics* 76 (3), pp. 337–68.

Index

Printed in the United States
by Baker & Taylor Publisher Services